SAMUEL PEPYS

AND THE

ROYAL NAVY

SAMUEL PEPYS

AND THE

ROYAL NAVY

LEES KNOWLES LECTURES DELIVERED
AT TRINITY COLLEGE IN CAMBRIDGE,
6, 13, 20 AND 27 NOVEMBER, 1919

BY

J. R. TANNER, Litt.D.

FELLOW OF ST JOHN'S COLLEGE

CAMBRIDGE
AT THE UNIVERSITY PRESS
1920

CAMBRIDGE
UNIVERSITY PRESS

University Printing House, Cambridge CB2 8BS, United Kingdom

Published in the United States of America by Cambridge University Press, New York

Cambridge University Press is part of the University of Cambridge.

It furthers the University's mission by disseminating knowledge in the pursuit of education, learning and research at the highest international levels of excellence.

www.cambridge.org
Information on this title: www.cambridge.org/9781107626430

First published 1920
First paperback edition 2013

A catalogue record for this publication is available from the British Library

ISBN 978-1-107-62643-0 Paperback

PREFACE

IN 1919 the writer was appointed by the Master and Fellows of Trinity College, Cambridge, Lees Knowles Lecturer in Military and Naval History for the academical year 1919–20, and the lectures are now printed almost exactly in the form in which they were delivered in November, 1919.

The object of the Lecturer was to present in a convenient form the general conclusions about the administration of the Royal Navy from the Restoration to the Revolution arrived at in the introductory volume of his *Catalogue of Pepysian Manuscripts*, published by the Navy Records Society in 1903 with a dedication, in the two hundredth year after his death, 'to the memory of Samuel Pepys, a great public servant.' The evidence there collected shews that Pepys, familiar to the last generation in the sphere of literature, was also a leading figure in an entirely different world, who rendered inestimable services to naval administration in spite of the peculiar difficulties under which he worked. These conclusions, with a part of the evidence on which they depend, are summarised in the present volume.

Thanks are due to the Master and Fellows of Trinity College for encouraging the enterprise; to the Council of the Navy Records Society for permission to use the material already published in the Society's series; to the Delegates of the Oxford Clarendon Press for allowing the author to use and quote from his Introduction to the reprint of Pepys's *Memoires of the Royal Navy*, 1679–88, issued in the Tudor and Stuart Library in 1906; and to Messrs Sidgwick and Jackson for a similar permission to use the Introduction to the section on 'Sea Manuscripts' in *Bibliotheca Pepysiana*.

J. R. T.

February, 1920.

CONTENTS

LECTURE I

INTRODUCTORY

THE materials for the administrative history of the Royal Navy from the Restoration to the Revolution are largely contributed by Cambridge.

The section of the Pepysian Library at Magdalene which Samuel Pepys classified as 'Sea Manuscripts' contains 114 volumes, the contents of which cover a wide field of naval history. Pepys's leading motive in collecting these is probably to be found in his projected 'History of the Navy.' Early in his career he thought of writing a 'History of the Dutch War,' 'it being a thing I much desire, and sorts mightily with my genius.'[1] Later on the design expanded into a complete naval history, upon which, at the time of his death, he was supposed to have been engaged for many years. Evelyn writes in his *Diary* on 26 May, 1703: 'This day died Mr Samuel Pepys, a very worthy, industrious, and curious person, none in England exceeding him in knowledge of the navy....He had for divers years under his hand the History of the Navy, or *Navalia* as he called it; but how far advanced, and what will follow of his, is left, I suppose, to his sister's son.' Pepys's correspondence with Evelyn and Sir William Dugdale suggests that it would have included in its scope the antiquities of the Navy and possibly the history of navigation, as well as administrative history; and this view is supported by his selection of 'sea' manuscripts for his Library.

---

[1] *Diary*, 13 June, 1664.

These manuscripts may be roughly classified in three groups :

(i) Official documents of Pepys's own time, the presence of which in the Library may be explained by the predatory habits of retiring officials in his day. Among these are to be found collections of real importance for the administrative history of the navy during his time, such as (1) *Naval and Admiralty Precedents* from 1660 to 1688—described as 'a collection of naval forms and other papers, serving for information and precedents in most of the principal occasions of the Admiralty and Navy calling for the same'; (2) *Admiralty Letters*, 14 volumes containing the whole of the ordinary correspondence which passed out of Pepys's office during his two Secretaryships, 1673-1679 and 1684-1688[1]—the equivalent of the modern letter-copying books, but in those days transcribed afresh with laborious care by a staff of clerks; (3) the *Admiralty Journal*, the minute-book of the Commission of the Admiralty from 1674 to 1679; (4) *Naval Minutes*, a volume in which Pepys made miscellaneous memoranda, many of them notes for his projected History; and (5) the *Navy White Book*, in which he noted abuses in shorthand, and wrote down what he called 'matters for future reflection' arising out of the Second Dutch War.

(ii) A second group of papers consists of official and unofficial documents—many of them acquired or copied at some expense—brought together deliberately in order to serve as material for the projected 'History of the Navy.' These include (1) a copy of Sir William Monson's *Naval Discourses*; (2) copious extracts from naval authorities and historians carefully indexed; (3) Penn's *Naval Collections*, being 'a collection of several manuscripts, taken out of

---

[1] Vols. ii.–v. of these letters have been calendared already, and calendars of vols. vi. and vii. are in preparation : see the writer's *Catalogue of Pepysian MSS.* (Navy Records Society's Publications), vols. ii. and iii.

Sir William Penn's closet, relating to the affairs of the Navy';
(4) various volumes relating to shipbuilding and navigation,
including the curious and valuable work entitled *Fragments
of Ancient Shipwrightry* and Sir Anthony Deane's *Doctrine of
Naval Architecture.* This last contains delicate and elaborate
drawings of a ship of each rate, and Evelyn records in his
Diary under date 28 January, 1682, the remarkable impression which a sight of it made upon him : ' Mr Pepys, late
Secretary to the Admiralty, showed me a large folio containing the whole mechanic part and art of building royal
ships and men-of-war, made by Sir Anthony Deane, being
so accurate a piece from the very keel to the lead block,
rigging, guns, victualling, manning, and even to every indi-
vidual pin and nail, in a method so astonishing and curious,
with a draught, both geometrical and in perspective, and
several sections, that I do not think the world can shew the
like. I esteem this book as an extraordinary jewel.' There
also falls into this group (5) the large and important collection in eleven volumes entitled by Pepys *A Miscellany of
Matters Historical, Political, and Naval.* This contains
copies of 1438 documents, transcribed from various sources,
and ranging from a complete copy in 114 folio pages of
Sir Philip Meadows's work on the Sovereignty of the Seas
down to ' A true Copy of the Great Turke his Stile which
he most commonly writeth in His great Affaires.' They
include documents relating to naval abuses; papers concerning salutes and the history of the flag, shipbuilding,
victualling, and finance ; a number of patents, commissions,
and lists of ships; transcripts from the Black Book of the
Admiralty; and collections relating to the Shipwrights'
Company and to the Corporation of Trinity House.

(iii) The third group consists of books and papers which
specially appealed to Pepys's characteristic curiosity, and
have no direct bearing upon naval history. The line between

this and the second group cannot, however, be sharply drawn, as few of the 'Sea Manuscripts' are merely curious, and irrelevant to the history of the navy as Pepys himself interpreted it. The contents of this group are not important for our present purpose, but one interesting fact may be noted. The inclusion in the *Miscellanies* of papers relating to Sir William Petty's calculations and experiments, and of a copy of 'A Discourse made by Sir Robert Southwell before the Royal Society, 8 April, 1675, touching Water,' suggests that Pepys's scientific interests were genuine, and were not due, as has been suggested, to a desire to commend himself to Charles II.

It is fortunate for the student of naval administration during the Restoration period that the 'Sea Manuscripts' in the Pepysian Library include two 'Discourses'[1] upon naval abuses written at the beginning of the period, which enable us to understand some of the difficulties with which Pepys and his colleagues had to contend. The *Second Discourse* by John Hollond, in succession Paymaster, Commissioner, and Surveyor of the Navy under the Commonwealth Government, following a *First Discourse* of 1638, is dated 1659; and the *Discourse* by Sir Robert Slyngesbie, a royalist naval commander, made Comptroller of the Navy on the King's return, is dated 1660. These give us the criticisms of a Parliamentarian of administrative experience and those of a royalist of experience at sea, made at the Restoration and supplying an excellent groundwork for the study of the period which followed it.

There is no time to traverse the whole field of the *Discourses*, but certain points may be considered by way of illustration.

[1] See Hollond's *Discourses of the Navy*, ed. J. R. Tanner, published by the Navy Records Society in 1896. This volume also includes Slyngesbie's *Discourse of the Navy*.

1. They bring into relief the remarkable durability of naval abuses. John Hollond was not the first writer to denounce abuses in the navy. This had been a fruitful topic for anonymous writers long before his day, and if the scattered papers on the subject were collected they would constitute a complete literature. The charges begin at least as early as the time of Hawkyns, and one writer[1] accuses him of what has always been regarded as one of the more modern refinements of cheating—the manufacture of a complete set of false books and vouchers for the purpose of baffling enquiry. The Pepysian Library contains copies of a number of exposures ranging from 1587 to 1611. The Reports of the Commissions of 1608 and 1618, and in a lesser degree of that of 1626, are of special importance in the history of the evolution of fraud. Sir William Monson, who in 1635 'turned physician' and studied 'how to cure the malignant diseases of corruption' that had 'crept in and infected his Majesty's whole navy,'[2] assigns some passages in his *Naval Tracts* to naval abuses; and in 1636 the Earl of Northumberland, fresh from the experience of a naval command, denounces them in a state paper to the King in Council[3]. Hollond only develops in detail earlier themes, and Pepys, who thought very highly of his *Discourses*, 'they hitting the very diseases of the navy which we are troubled with now-a-days,'[4] takes up the same tale. And such is the tenacity of life exhibited by a well-established naval abuse, that a Parliamentary enquiry of 1783[5] into the Victualling Department at Portsmouth revealed malpractices of a kind very

[1] Pepysian MSS., *Miscellanies*, x. 273.
[2] *Naval Tracts* (ed. M. Oppenheim), iv. 143.
[3] See Appendix to Hollond's *Discourses*, pp. 361–406.
[4] *Diary*, 25 July, 1662.
[5] 'Interim Report of a Committee to inquire into abuses in the Victualling Department at Portsmouth' (*House of Commons Miscellaneous Reports*, vol. xxxvi. No. 55).

similar to those described by Hollond. The keys of the victualling storehouses had been entrusted to improper recipients, who had access to the stores at all hours; certain persons kept hogs in the King's storehouses, which were 'fed with the King's serviceable biscuit'; planks, spars, staves, and barrels were converted to private use; 'mops and brooms' from the store were appropriated by an official who 'kept a shop and dealt in those articles'; the King's wine was drawn off in large quantities ' in bottles in a clandestine manner'; certificates were granted for stores before they were actually received, and for articles received short, these being signed in blank by the clerk of the check beforehand; it was a 'common practice' to send in bags of bread deficient in weight; the accounts were imperfectly kept, and showed enormous deficiencies of stores; by collusion with the contractor stores were accepted that were ' of improper quality and not according to contract'; and the victualling board paid excessive prices to a bread contractor with whom they were in collusion and refused to allow others to tender.

2. Let me give you next a few illustrations of the kind of abuse which Hollond and his predecessors had pointed out, and with which Pepys and his colleagues had to deal.

(a) Hollond, like Pepys, appears to have had a genuine sympathy for the sorrows of the 'poor seaman,' and he complains bitterly of the long delays in paying wages ; the 'intolerable abuse to poor seamen in their wages' by naval captains 'who are of late turned merchants, and have and do lay magazines of clothes,...tobacco, strong waters, and such like commodities into their ships upon pretence of relieving poor seamen in their wants, but indeed for no other reason than their private profit'[1]; the practice of discharging sick men without adequate funds to take them home ;

[1] *Discourses*, p. 131.

and the payment of wages by tickets instead of cash, thus creating a depreciated paper currency.

(*b*) Hollond also speaks strongly against the practice of using the State's labour in the gardens or grounds of officials, and the State's materials in repairing private houses or sumptuously decorating official residences, 'by painting, paving, and other ornamental tricking.'[1] Here he attacks a longstanding abuse, for a writer of 1597 had already charged the Comptroller of the Navy with employing five labourers from the dockyard 'by the space of half a year' at his house at Chatham 'about the making of a bowling alley and planting of trees,'[2] and in 1603 Phineas Pett was accused of appropriating the King's timber 'to make a bridge into his meadow' and to set up 'posts to hang clothes on in his garden,' and also labour for the same[3]. It is true that Pett's accuser is not above suspicion, for he begins his philippic with an artless exposition of his motives: 'In the last year of the Queen's reign, I, seeing some abuses by Phineas Pett, told him he had not done his duty. He strook me with his cudgel. I told him he had been better he had held his hand, for he should pay for it.' Pett was in some respects a calumniated man, but this particular kind of peculation is more easily justified to the official conscience than any other, and there is nothing inherently improbable in the accusation.

(*c*) The combination of captains and pursers to return false musters, or to present men to receive pay who never served, was another longstanding abuse. There was in the navy a recognised system of drawing pay for non-existent persons to which no discredit attached, for it was the regular way of giving the officers extra pay. Thus the captains were allowed a 'dead pay' apiece on the sea-books 'for their

[1] *Discourses*, p. 149.

[2] *A Large and Severe Discourse*, &c. (Pepysian MSS., *Miscellanies*, x. 226).

[3] *A Large and Particular Complaint against Phineas Pett*, &c. (Pepysian MSS., *Miscellanies*, x. 257).

retines'; and in harbour no less than four varieties of dead
pay were recognised, including wages and victuals paid to
men for keeping ships 'which long since had no being.' We
also hear of an allowance demanded in the Narrow Seas
'for a preacher and his man, though no such devotion be
ever used on board.' The same principle appears in the
18th century in connexion with what were known as 'widows'
men.' The captain was authorised to enter one or two fic-
titious persons in every hundred men of his ship's complement, and the wages drawn in their names and the value
of the victuals to which they would have been entitled were
applied to the relief of the widows of officers and seamen
who had served in the navy[1]. In the 16th and 17th centuries,
however, the established principle was liable to a variety of
fraudulent applications. A paper of 1603 gives a circum-
stantial account of a case in which the companies of a
squadron of four ships were mustered, and it was found that
of 1250 men charged for, only 958 were actually serving,
the King being 'abused in the pay of 292 men, which for
four months, the least time of their employment,' was £800[2].
The Report of the Commission of 1608 explains how this
could happen, for 'the captains, being for the most part poor
gentlemen, did mend their fortunes by combining with the
pursers'[3]; and Hollond, in his *First Discourse*, urges as a
remedy 'an increase of means from the King' for 'all
subordinate ministers acting in the navy,' since 'for want
thereof' they are 'necessitated to one of these two particulars, either to live knaves or die beggars—and sometimes
to both.'[4]

[1] *Discourses*, p. 140 *n*.
[2] *An Account of Particular Abuses to be proved against the Officers of the Navy* (Pepysian MSS., *Miscellanies*, x. 271).
[3] C. N. Robinson, *The British Fleet*, p. 347. There are two copies of the Report of 1608 in the Pepysian Library—MSS. 2165, and *Miscellanies*, iii. 355.
[4] *Discourses*, p. 100.

(*d*) The danger of collusion among officials was one of the chief difficulties in the way of would-be reformers, and just as collusion between the captains and the pursers defrauded the King in the matter of pay, so collusion between the victuallers and the pursers defrauded the King over the provision of victuals. Sir William Monson, in his *Naval Tracts*, gives instances of such collusion, and shews how easily it can be managed. Thus the victualler and the purser would contract between themselves for the purser to be allowed to victual a certain number of men on board each ship, paying the victualler for the privilege but making his own profit on the victuals he supplied. 'Which,' says Monson, 'besides that it breeds a great inconvenience, for the purser's unreasonable griping the sailors of their victuals, and plucking it, as it were, out of their bellies, it makes them become weak, sick, and feeble, and then follows an infection and inability to do their labour, or else uproars, mutinies, and disorders ensue among the company.'[1] Even if the officers of the ship did their duty, it was sometimes the case that the higher authorities ashore intervened from corrupt motives. Monson tells us that when the *James* was taking in victuals in Tilbury Hope, 'there appeared a certain proportion of beef and pork able with its scent to have poisoned the whole company, but by the carefulness of the quartermasters it was found unserviceable. Yet after it was refused by the said officers of the ship, and lay upon the hatches unstowed, some of the Officers of the Navy repaired aboard and, by their authority and great anger, forced it to be taken in for good victuals....My observation to this point is that, though the Officers of the Navy have nothing to do with the victualling part, yet it is likely there is a combination betwixt the one and the other, like to a mayor of a corporation, a baker, who for that year will favour the brewer

[1] *Naval Tracts*, iv. 147.

that shall the next year do the like to his trade when he becomes mayor.'[1] Hollond's remedy for these abuses was to abolish the victualling contractor altogether, and for the State to take over the victualling by means of a victualling department[2]. This system of victualling 'upon account,' as it was called, was actually adopted from 1655 to the Restoration, and again after 1683; but the difficulties were not altogether met by the change, for the officials who victualled 'upon account' were liable to collusion with the vendors of victuals from whom they bought, and in this case the King's service suffered in a different way.

(e) The administrative defects of the victualling recurred on almost as serious a scale in the department of stores, and great complaints are made, both by John Hollond and the earlier writers, of the bad quality of cordage and timber and of the frauds connected with their purveyance. Cordage would be entered by the storekeeper as heavier than it weighed; old cordage would be sold at absurdly low prices to the minor officials of the dockyard; and materials still fit for service would be condemned as unserviceable by an official who himself acted as a contractor for purchasing unserviceable stores[3]. The inefficiency of the surveyors of timber led them to purchase bad materials[4], and their dishonesty provoked them to glut the King's stores with defective timber at exorbitant prices[5] in order to favour the monopolist or merchant with whom they were in profitable collusion.

The worst and most corrupt period of naval administration was the reign of James I, and by the Restoration the navy was on a higher plane of efficiency and honesty; but the criticisms of such writers as Hollond and Slyngesbie shew

---

[1] *Naval Tracts*, iv. 143.   [2] *Discourses*, p. 154.
[3] Pepysian MSS., No. 2735, p. 65.
[4] Hollond, *First Discourse* (*Discourses*, p. 78).   [5] *Ib.* p. 67.

how much remained for the reformer to do. It is remarkable that the period of the later Stuarts, so deeply sunk in political corruption, produced a great naval organizer and reformer in the person of Samuel Pepys.

There are 17 different ways of spelling the Diarist's name, but only three of pronouncing it. The descendants of his sister Paulina, now represented by the family of Pepys Cockerell, pronounce it *Peeps*; this is also the established tradition at Magdalene, and is probably the way in which Samuel himself pronounced it. The branch of the Pepys family which is now represented by the Earl of Cottenham, pronounce their name *Peppis*. The British public calls it *Peps*, and this is the only pronunciation in favour of which there is no family or other tradition. An epigram contributed to the *Graphic* in November, 1891, not only comes to a wrong conclusion about the pronunciation, but is also full of misleading statements about the man:

> There are people, I'm told—some say there are heaps—
> Who speak of the talkative Samuel as Peeps;
> And some, so precise and pedantic their step is,
> Who call the delightful old Diarist, Pepys;
> But those I think right, and I follow their steps,
> Ever mention the garrulous gossip as Peps.

But is he nothing more than 'the talkative Samuel,' 'the delightful old Diarist,' 'the garrulous gossip'? Even 'old' is the wrong epithet unless it is restricted to historical antiquity, for Pepys was not 27 when he began the *Diary*[1], and only 36 when the partial failure of his eyesight compelled him, to his great regret, to give it up, 'which is almost as much as to see myself go into my grave.'[2] Yet he lived to be 70 years of age, and although for part of his career he

---

[1] On 1 January, 1660.   [2] *Diary*, 31 May, 1669.

was out of office, he certainly became, what Monck had called him earlier with exaggerated compliment, 'the right hand of the navy.'[1] The maturity of his powers lies outside the period of the *Diary*, and it is his later life that makes good his claim to be regarded as one of the best public officials who ever served the State. In fact, Pepys's *Diary* is only a by-product of the life of Samuel Pepys.

Nevertheless the *Diary*, in spite of its infinite accumulations of unimportant detail, and its conscientious record of small vices, shews us the great official in the making. Let me give two illustrations, one on the lower levels of the *Diary* and the other where it reaches its highest plane.

30 May, 1660: 'All this morning making up my accounts, in which I counted that I had made myself now worth about £80, at which my heart was glad and blessed God.' 3 June, 1660: 'At sermon in the morning; after dinner into my cabin to cast my accounts up, and find myself to be worth near £100, for which I bless Almighty God, it being more than I hoped for so soon.' 5 September, 1660: 'In the evening, my wife being a little impatient, I went along with her to buy her a necklace of pearl, which will cost £4. 10s., which I am willing to comply with her in for her encouragement, and because I have lately got money, having now above £200 cash beforehand in the world. Home, and having in our way bought a rabbit and two little lobsters, my wife and I did sup late, and so to bed.' This methodical care in calculating ways and means and recording expenditure, when applied to the greater affairs of the navy, appears as a habit of method and order, and a remarkable instinct for business. Pepys introduced into a slipshod and rather chaotic organisation a high degree of system and method, and so vastly increased its efficiency in every direction.

[1] *Diary*, 24 April, 1665.

My other illustration is from the account given in the *Diary* of the funeral of Sir Christopher Myngs, who had been mortally wounded in action on the last day of the great battle with the Dutch off the North Foreland, June 1–4, 1666. Pepys was present at the funeral in a coach with Sir William Coventry, at which, he tells us[1], 'there happened this extraordinary case—one of the most romantique that ever I heard of in my life, and could not have believed but that I did see it; which was this:—About a dozen able, lusty, proper men come to the coach-side with tears in their eyes, and one of them that spoke for the rest begun and says to Sir W. Coventry, "We are here a dozen of us that have long known and loved and served our dead commander, Sir Christopher Mings, and have now done the last office of laying him in the ground. We would be glad we had any other to offer after him, and in revenge of him. All we have is our lives; if you will please to get his Royal Highness to give us a fireship among us all, here is a dozen of us, out of all which choose you one to be commander, and the rest of us, whoever he is, will serve him; and, if possible, do that that shall show our memory of our dead commander, and our revenge." Sir W. Coventry was herewith much moved (as well as I, who could hardly abstain from weeping), and took their names, and so parted; telling me he would move his Royal Highness as in a thing very extraordinary, which was done.' No more touching tribute than this has ever been paid to the memory of a great seaman, nor better evidence given of the simple loyalty of sea-faring men which in their descendants has served us so well of late. 'The truth is,' continues Pepys, 'Sir Christopher Mings was a very stout man, and a man of great parts, and most excellent tongue among ordinary

---

[1] *Diary*, 13 June, 1666.

men....He had brought his family into a way of being great;
but dying at this time, his memory and name...will be quite
forgot in a few months as if he had never been, nor any of
his name be the better by it; he having not had time to will
any estate, but is dead poor rather than rich.' A writer who
could describe such a scene in a style which comes so near
distinction, and could then reflect with dignity upon the
swift passing of human greatness, is something more than
a '.delightful old Diarist' or a 'garrulous gossip'; but it is
characteristic of Pepys that he should thus conclude his
entry for the day: 'In my way home I called on a fisherman
and bought three eeles, which cost me three shillings.'

I have quoted this passage about the funeral of Sir Christopher Myngs for another reason—it enables us to understand
how Pepys developed later on so impressive an official style.
He takes pleasure in long, labyrinthine sentences, in which
the thread of thought winds deviously through an infinity of
dependent clauses, but the thread is never lost, and the reader
always arrives in the end at the destined goal. He has a dis-
criminating taste in the selection of words, always choosing
the more impressive, and leaving the reader with the sense
of something dignified moving before him, like a procession,
but never sacrificing clearness and precision to mere sound.
Yet associated with all this pomp is a sense of humour,
usually full-flavoured, but on occasion as subtle and delicate
as need be[1], and finding its way even into the more dismal
kinds of official correspondence.

To illustrate the point of complexity, let me read you a
letter to the Navy Board of 2 June, 1677, which I came

---

[1] See for instance a letter of 17 December, 1678, courteously discouraging a
commander from sending his chaplain's sermon to the Bishop of London for
his perusal, as owing to the pressing nature of his Parliamentary engagements
the Bishop might not be 'at leisure to overlook it' (Pepysian MSS., *Admiralty
Letters*, viii. 432).

across not long ago among the Pepysian papers[1]. It consists of a single colossal sentence, yet the meaning is perfectly clear. If you want a parallel, you should go to the Prayer Book, to the Exhortation which precedes the General Confession; for this, although punctuated as three sentences, is structurally only one.

There being a prospect (as you will know) of a considerable number of great ships to be built, and many applications being already, and more likely to be yet made to his Majesty and my Lords of the Admiralty for employments by persons so far from having merited the same by any past service as to be wholly strangers to the business thereof, or at least have their qualifications for the same wholly unknown, nor have any title to his Majesty's favour therein more than their interest (which possibly they have bought too) in the persons they solicit by, And knowing that it is his Majesty's royal intentions, as well as for the benefit of his service, that the employments arising upon his ships be disposed to such as by their long and faithful services and experiences are best fitted for and deserve the same, I make it my desire to you that you will at your first convenience cause the list of the present standing officers of his Majesty's fleet, namely, pursers, boatswains, and carpenters, to be overlooked, and a collection thence made of such as by length of service, frequency and strictness of passing their accounts, together with their diligence and sobriety, you shall find most deserving to be advanced from lesser ships to bigger, transmitting the same to me in order to my laying it (as there shall be occasion) before his Majesty for the benefit of the persons you shall therein do right to and encouragement of others to imitate them in deserving well in his service, Towards the obtaining of which I shall by the grace of God endeavour constantly to do my part, as I doubt not you will also do yours, putting in execution the Lord Admiral's instructions for informing yourselves well in the good and bad behaviour of these officers, and particularly by your enquiries after the same at pays, when by the presence of the ship's companies the same will most probably be understood.

The reputation of Samuel Pepys has suffered in two ways. Readers of the *Diary* under-estimate him because they con-

---

[1] Pepysian MSS., *Admiralty Letters*, vi. 43.

ceive of him as a diarist only, and do not realize the serious-
ness of his public responsibilities or the greatness of his
official career. On the other hand, naval historians have
often under-estimated him because they have failed to appreciate the difficulties with which he had to contend. If these
difficulties are allowed for, the services rendered by Samuel
Pepys to the navy are incomparable. He stood for a vigorous
shipbuilding policy, for methodical organisation in every
department, and for the restoration of a lost naval discipline.
This was recognised by his immediate posterity, and in the
century after his death a great tradition grew up about his
name. A commission which reported in 1805 spoke of him
as 'a man of extraordinary knowledge in all that related to
the business' of the navy, 'of great talents, and the most
indefatigable industry.' The respect paid to his authority
by the generation of naval administrators which succeeded
his own—comparable only perhaps to the weight which
Lord Chief Justice Coke had carried among the lawyers of
an earlier time—led to a number of transcripts being made
from the Pepysian manuscripts and preserved in the Admiralty Library for the guidance of his successors. And this
tradition has to be reconciled with the other and widely
different tradition associated with the Pepys of the *Diary*.

It is not easy to realise that the two traditions belong to
the same person. It is extraordinary that a man should
have written the *Diary*, but it is much more extraordinary
that the man who wrote the *Diary* should also have been
'the right hand of the navy.' From the *Diary* we learn that
Pepys was a musician, a dandy, a collector of books and
prints, an observer of boundless curiosity, and, as a critic
has pointed out, one who possessed an 'amazing zest for
life.' From the Pepysian manuscripts we learn that he was
a man of sound judgment, of orderly and methodical business habits, of great administrative capacity and energy;

and that he possessed extraordinary shrewdness and tact in dealing with men. At certain points in the *Diary* we can see the great official maturing, but in the main the intimate self-revelation of a human being seems far removed from official life. It is the combination of qualities that is so astounding, and those who regard Pepys only as 'the most amusing and capable of our seventeenth century diarists '[1]— a mere literary performer making sport for us—do little justice to a great career.

[1] Historical MSS. Commission, *Fifteenth Report*, Appendix, pt. ii. p. 153.

LECTURE II

ADMINISTRATION

THE history of naval administration between the Restoration and the Revolution falls naturally into four periods: (1) 1660–73, from the appointment of the Duke of York to be Lord High Admiral, until his retirement after the passing of the Test Act; (2) 1673–79, the first Secretaryship of Samuel Pepys; (3) 1679–84, the period of administrative disorder which followed his resignation; and (4) 1684–88, from the return of the Duke of York to office until the Revolution—this period being also that of Pepys's second Secretaryship.

At the date of the King's Restoration the direction of the navy was in the hands of an Admiralty Commission of twenty-eight, appointed by the restored Rump Parliament in December, 1659[1], with a Navy Board of seven experts under it. One of the earlier acts of Charles II on his return was to dissolve these two bodies, and to revive the ancient form of navy government by a Lord High Admiral and four Principal Officers—the Treasurer, the Comptroller, the Surveyor, and the Clerk of the Acts. James, Duke of York, the King's brother, afterwards James II, was made Lord High Admiral—an appointment which realised the ideas of Monson, who had written earlier: 'The way to settle things is to appoint an Admiral, young, heroical, and of a great blood. His experience in sea affairs is not so much to be required at first as his sincerity, honour, and wisdom; for his daily practice in his Office, with conference of able and experienced

---

[1] A list of Lord High Admirals and Admiralty Commissions from August, 1628, to March, 1689, is given in Pepysian MSS., *Miscellanies*, xi. 211–26.

men, will quickly instruct him.'[1] All the Stuarts were in-
terested in the sea. Nothing gave Charles II more pleasure
than to sail down the Thames in one of his yachts to inspect
his ships, and his brother possessed something like an expert knowledge of naval affairs. Even Macaulay, who has
scarcely a good word to say for him, allows that he would
have made 'a respectable clerk in the dockyard at Chatham.'[2]
He was an authority on shipbuilding questions[3], and Pepys,
in a private minute not intended for publication and therefore likely to express his real mind, ascribes much of the
strength of the navy in his day to the Duke's energy in
'getting ships to be begun to be built, in confidence that
when they were begun they would not let them want finish-
ing, who otherwise would never of themselves have spared
money from lesser uses to begin to build.'[4] He was also by
temperament stiff in discipline, and threw his influence
strongly on the side of reform. The numerous references to
him in the State Papers shew that while he was Lord High
Admiral he bestowed a great deal of attention upon the
duties of the office[5].

The new Treasurer of the Navy was Sir George Carteret,
who, entering the service as a boy, had risen to high command in the navy, and had served as Comptroller in the
reign of Charles I. 'Besides his other parts of honesty and

---

[1] *Naval Tracts*, iv. 141.

[2] *History of England* (2 vols. Longman, 1880), i. 218.

[3] Pepysian MSS., *Admiralty Letters*, xii. 71. We also find him desiring 'for
his own satisfaction and use to have an account of the just rake of all the up-
right-stemmed ships in his royal navy, and the present seat of the step of each
main-mast' (*ib.* xi. 200); and his pocket-book in the Pepysian Library (MSS.
No. 488) contains a number of facts about the navy. For his interest in inven-
tions see *Admiralty Letters*, xii. 91 and xiii. 23.

[4] Pepysian MSS. No. 2866, *Naval Minutes*, p. 175.

[5] *Calendar of State Papers, Domestic*, 1667–8, p. xxxvi; *cf.* also *Diary*, 8 July,
1668 ('I to the Duke of York to attend him about the business of the Office;
and find him mighty free to me, and how he is concerned to mend things in the
Navy himself, and not leave it to other people').

discretion,' says Clarendon, he was 'undoubtedly as good, if not the best, seaman in England,'[1] and Sir William Coventry, his consistent opponent, described him to Pepys as 'a man that do take the most pains, and gives himself the most to do business of any about the Court, without any desire of pleasure or divertisements.'[2] Pepys himself wrote of him not long before his fall: 'I do take' him 'for a most honest man.'[3]

Sir Robert Slyngesbie, the new Comptroller, was himself the son of a Comptroller of the Navy, and had served as a sea-captain as early as 1633[4], having been 'from his infancy bred up and employed in the navy.'[5]

Sir William Batten, the Surveyor, was only returning to an office which he had already held, for he had been Surveyor of the Navy from 1638 to 1642, and afterwards an active naval commander. Pepys began by borrowing £40 of him[6], and then came to dislike him. Their relations were not improved by the small social jealousies which broke out between their wives. Lady Batten complained to Pepys that 'there was not the neighbourliness between her' and Mrs Pepys 'that was fit to be'; that Mrs Pepys spoke 'unhandsomely of her,' and her maid 'mocked her' over the garden wall[7]. Soon after, Pepys records with some satisfaction that he and his wife managed to take precedence of Lady Batten in going out of church, 'which I believe will vex her.'[8] What the *Diary* calls a 'fray' eventually took place between the two ladies, and Lady Batten was 'mighty high upon it,' telling Mrs Pepys's 'boy' that 'she would teach his mistress better manners, which my wife answered

[1] *Dictionary of National Biography*, ix. 208.
[2] *Diary*, 30 October, 1662.   [3] *Ib.* 12 April, 1667.
[4] *Calendar of State Papers, Domestic*, 1631–3, p. 546.
[5] *State Papers, Domestic, Charles II*, i. 153.
[6] *Diary*, 31 July, 1661.
[7] *Ib.* 5 November, 1662.   [8] *Ib.* 28 December, 1662.

aloud that she might hear, that she could learn little manners of her."[1] Pepys came to the conclusion that his wife
was to blame[2]. Sir William Batten, who does not deserve
the treatment he meets with in the *Diary*, had at first
done what he could to accommodate the quarrel, saying to
Pepys that 'he desired the difference between our wives
might not make a difference between us,'[3] but quarrels of
this kind are the hardest of all to compose, and it is not to
the *Diary* that Batten's biographer goes for his facts. Pepys
calls him a knave[4] and a sot[5], and accuses him of 'corruption
and underhand dealing'[6]; and in reviewing his own position
on the last day of the year 1663, he writes: 'At the Office
I am well, though envied to the devil by Sir William Batten,
who hates me to death, but cannot hurt me. The rest either
love me, or at least do not shew otherwise....' The news of
Batten's last illness was, however, received with some sign
of relenting. 'Word is brought me that he is so ill that it is
believed he cannot live till to-morrow, which troubles me
and my wife mightily, partly out of kindness, he being
a good neighbour—and partly because of the money he
owes me upon our bargain of the late prize.'[7]

The only one of the Principal Officers who knew nothing
about the navy was the Clerk of the Acts, Samuel Pepys
himself. He obtained the office by the influence of his
patron, Edward Mountagu, the first Earl of Sandwich, a
distinguished naval commander, who was first cousin to
Pepys's father and recognised the claims of kinship after the
fashion of his day. It was necessary first to buy out Thomas
Barlow, who had been Clerk of the Acts under Charles I, and
Pepys, observing that he was 'an old, consumptive man,'[8]

---

[1] *Diary*, 10 March, 1663.   [2] *Ib.* 11 March, 1663.
[3] *Ib.* 25 July, 1662.   [4] *Ib.* 5 July, 1664.
[5] *Ib.* 23 May, 1664.   [6] *Ib.* 13 June, 1663.
[7] *Ib.* 4 October, 1667.   [8] *Ib.* 17 July, 1660.

offered him £100 a year. He lived until 1665, and then a
characteristic entry appears in the *Diary*. ' At noon home
to dinner, and then to my office again, where Sir William
Petty comes among other things to tell me that Mr Barlow
is dead; for which, God knows my heart, I could be as sorry
as is possible for one to be for a stranger by whose death
he gets £100 per annum, he being a worthy, honest man;
but after having considered that, when I come to consider
the providence of God by this means unexpectedly to give
me £100 a year more in my estate, I have cause to bless
God, and do it from the bottom of my heart.'[1]

Besides the four Principal Officers, the new Navy Board
also included three extra Commissioners of the Navy, Lord
Berkeley, Sir William Penn, and Peter Pett. Lord Berkeley
was a distinguished soldier, who had won great honour at
Stratton, and had served under Turenne from 1652 to 1655[2].
Sir William Penn was the son of a seaman and had been a
seaman all his life. He had been rear-admiral and then
vice-admiral in the time of the Long Parliament; he had
served as vice-admiral under Blake, had commanded the
expedition which seized Jamaica[3], and had been a member
of two Admiralty Commissions during the Interregnum[4].
Peter Pett came of a famous family of shipbuilders[5]—an
earlier Pett had been master shipwright at Deptford in the
reign of Edward VI[6]—and he had already served as resident
Commissioner at Chatham for thirteen years[7]. Pett occupied
a somewhat inferior position to his colleagues, as he was
required still to reside at Chatham to take charge of the
dockyard there—at this time the most important of the royal

[1] *Diary*, 9 February, 1665.
[2] *Dictionary of National Biography*, iv. 361–2.   [3] *Ib.* xliv. 308–9.
[4] The Commissions of 1653 and 1659 (Pepysian MSS., *Miscellanies*, xi. 216,
218, 219).
[5] *Dictionary of National Biography*, xlv. 103.   [6] *Ib.* xlv. 102.
[7] H. B. Wheatley, *Samuel Pepys and the World he lived in*, p. 285.

yards, described in the *Admiralty Letters* as 'the master-yard of all the rest.'[1] The other two Commissioners had no special duties assigned to them, and this was regarded as one of the advantages of the system now established, since they were 'not limited to any, and yet furnished with powers of acting and controlling every part, both of the particular and common duties of the Office'...'understanding the defects of the whole, and applying their assistance where it may be most useful.'[2]

It will be observed that on the Navy Board of the Restoration expert experience was overwhelmingly repre-sented. Of its seven members four were seamen; one a soldier—and it must be remembered that at this time the line between the two services was not distinctly drawn, for Blake had been a lieutenant-colonel and Monck commander-in-chief of an army before they were appointed to command fleets as 'generals-at-sea'; one represented experience of shipbuilding and dockyard administration; and only the Clerk of the Acts knew nothing about the sea. Sir Walter Ralegh had remarked in his day: 'It were to be wished that the chief officers under the Lord Admiral...should be men of the best experience in sea-service,' and had com-plained that sometimes 'by the special favour of princes' or 'the mediation of great men for the preferment of their servants,' or 'now and then by virtue of the purse,' persons 'very raw and ignorant' are 'very unworthily and unfitly nominated to those places.'[3] But such criticisms applied no longer. The King had made a good choice of fit persons duly qualified, and had established a naval administration which, if it failed, would not fail for lack of knowledge.

---

[1] x. 358.
[2] *Report of the Navy Commissioners to the Duke of York*, 17 April, 1669; printed in Charnock, *Marine Architecture*, ii. 406.
[3] *Observations on the Navy and Sea Service* (*Works*, viii. 336).

There were a good many subsequent changes, but the
importance of administration by experts was not again lost
sight of. The office of Treasurer of the Navy soon fell to
the men of accounts, and in 1667 Sir George Carteret was
succeeded by the Earl of Anglesey, a 'laborious, skilful,
cautious, moderate' official, who had had seven years' experience of finance as Vice-Treasurer and Receiver-General
for Ireland[1]. But with this exception, if the post of a Principal Officer was vacated by a naval expert it was offered
to a naval expert again. When Sir Robert Slyngesbie, the
Comptroller, died in 1661[2], he was succeeded by Sir John
Mennes, who had served under Sir William Monson in the
Narrow Seas, and had had a wide experience of the navy[3].
This appointment was not as successful as might have been
expected. Pepys thought him 'most excellent pleasant company'[4] and 'a very good, harmless, honest gentleman,'[5] but
he is always attacking his incapacity[6], and refers to him on
one occasion as a 'doating fool.'[7] On his death in 1671 the
office passed to Sir Thomas Allin, originally a shipowner at
Lowestoft, who had served under Prince Rupert, and had
acquired a reputation in the Second Dutch War[8]. When
Sir William Batten, the Surveyor, died in 1667, he was succeeded by Colonel Thomas Middleton, who had been resident
Commissioner at Portsmouth[9]; and when in 1672 Middleton

[1] *Dictionary of National Biography*, ii. 2–3.
[2] 'So home again, and in the evening news was brought that Sir R. Slingsby,
our Comptroller, (who hath this day been sick a week) is dead; which put me
into so great trouble of mind that all the night I could not sleep, he being a
man that loved me, and had many qualities that made me love him above all
the Officers and Commissioners in the Navy' (*Diary*, 26 October, 1661).
[3] *Dictionary of National Biography*, xxxvii. 253–4.
[4] *Diary*, 2 January, 1666.   [5] *Ib.* 20 August, 1666.
[6] *Ib.* 7 April, 1663; 5 October, 1663; 6 October, 1666; 4 January, 1669.
[7] *Ib.* 2 April, 1664.
[8] *Dictionary of National Biography*, i. 332.
[9] Pepys joined with Penn in recommending him as 'a most honest and understanding man, and fit for that place' (*Diary*, 5 October, 1667).

was transferred to Chatham, John Tippetts, who had followed him at Portsmouth, was appointed to the Surveyor-
ship[1]. It should be noticed that whereas during the thirteen
years of naval history from 1660 to 1673 the office of Treasurer of the Navy was held by four different persons, and the
offices of Comptroller and Surveyor each by three, there was
no change in the office of Clerk of the Acts. Pepys was
the only one of the Principal Officers whose experience
was continuous.

The extra Commissionerships, when vacancies arose, did
not all go to naval experts, but men of ability were selected
for them, and sometimes men of distinction. When in 1662
another extra Commissioner was appointed, the choice fell
on William Coventry, a civilian; but Coventry had already
had two years' experience of naval administration as Secretary to the Lord High Admiral, and his ability soon made
him one of the most valuable members of the Navy Board.
Burnet described him in 1665 as 'a man of great actions
and eminent virtues'; Temple credits him with high political
capacity; Evelyn calls him 'a wise and witty gentleman'[2];
and the *Diary* shews how warmly Pepys was attached to
him[3]. In 1664 an extra Commissionership was conferred
on Lord Brouncker, a literary man, an intimate friend of
Evelyn's, and the first President of the Royal Society, who
took something more than an amateur's interest in shipbuilding, and in 1662 had built a yacht for the King[4]. Pepys could
not make up his mind about him; for in 1667 he speaks of
him as 'a rotten-hearted, false man as any else I know, even
as Sir W. Penn himself, and therefore I must beware of him

[1] *Calendar of State Papers, Domestic*, 1672, p. 551.
[2] *Dictionary of National Biography*, xii. 363.
[3] *E.g.* 14 September, 1662 ('found him to admiration good and industrious,
and I think my most true friend in all things that are fair'); 18 November, 1662
('I am still in love more and more with him for his real worth'); and elsewhere.
[4] *Dictionary of National Biography*, vi. 470.

accordingly, and I hope I shall,'[1] and in 1668 he regards
him as the best man in the Navy Office[2]. One of the extra
Commissioners, Sir Edward Seymour, was also Speaker of
the House of Commons.

The Navy Board was by tradition the Lord High Admiral's council of advice for that part of his office which
was concerned with the government of the navy, and Monson
alludes to its members as 'the conduit pipes to whom the
Lord Admiral properly directs all his commands for his
Majesty's service, and from whom it descends to all other
inferior officers and ministers under them whatsoever.'[3] In
practice the Board enjoyed very large administrative powers,
for it was authorised 'to cause all ordinary businesses to be
done according to the ancient and allowed practice of the
Office, and extraordinary according to the warrants and
directions from the Lord Admiral and the State '[4]; but in
theory it existed only in order to carry out the general instructions which the Duke of York had issued early in 1662[5],
not long after he had taken office. These were drawn in
comprehensive terms, and of necessity left a vast number of
decisions on particular questions to be taken by the Board.
These instructions of 1662 remained in force until the
Admiralty was reorganised at the beginning of the 19th
century[6].

It is evident that the administration of the navy after the
Restoration was in the hands of able and experienced men,

---

[1] *Diary*, 29 January, 1667.   [2] *Ib.* 25 August, 1668.

[3] *Naval Tracts*, iii. 398.

[4] Pepysian MSS. No. 2611, Sir William Penn's *Collections*, p. 4.

[5] These were founded upon earlier instructions issued in 1640 by the Earl of
Northumberland when Lord High Admiral. They were printed in 1717 from
an imperfect copy under the title *The Œconomy of H.M.'s Navy Office*, but
there are two complete copies in the Pepysian Library, one among *Naval
Precedents* (No. 2867, pp. 356–98) and the other in Sir William Penn's *Collections* (No. 2611, pp. 127–90).

[6] H. B. Wheatley, *Samuel Pepys and the World he lived in*, p. 138.

and that they were acting under instructions which were good enough to survive without material alteration for another century and a half. Yet there is abundant evidence in the Pepysian manuscripts and elsewhere to shew that naval administration during the period 1660–1673 was in the main a disastrous failure. The reason why the collapse was so complete was the pressure of the Second Dutch War upon the resources of the naval administration, but the essential causes lay deeper than external events. First and foremost undoubtedly stands the problem of finance. The want of money was the root of all evil in the Stuart navy. I propose to deal fully with this problem·in my next lecture, and will only ask you to note its existence now. But there was more than this. On 15 August, 1666, Pepys made a remarkable entry in the *Diary* which I think gives the key to the situation: 'Thence walked over the Park with Sir W. Coventry, in our way talking of the unhappy state of our Office; and I took an opportunity to let him know, that though the backwardnesses of all our matters of the Office may be well imputed to the known want of money, yet perhaps there might be personal and particular failings.' He then notes Coventry's reply, which indicates the way in which personal failings were themselves affected by want of money. 'Nor, indeed, says he, is there room now-a-days to find fault with any particular man, while we are in this condition for money.' The whole service was breathing the miasmas exhaled by a corrupt Court. Slackness was fashionable because the King was slack, and the higher naval administration had to contend with idleness and dishonesty in the lower ranks of the service due to a relaxation of the standards of public and private duty. In this conflict it was at a serious disadvantage, for it was impossible effectively to control subordinates whom there was no money to pay. The members of the Navy Board were capable and experienced, and their intentions were excellent, but the atmosphere was poisonous and the situation beyond control. 'Personal and particular failings' in combination with financial disorder ruined the Navy Office, as they would have ruined any public department in any country and at any time.

It would be idle to pretend that the Restoration officials conformed to modern standards of official purity; although they were very much better than the corrupt administrators of the reign of James I. Pepys is convicted on his own confession of a good deal that would be unthinkable to-day. During the period of the *Diary* his salary as Clerk of the Acts was £350 a year; while in 1665 he was appointed Treasurer of the Tangier Commission, and from 1665 to 1667 he was Surveyor-General of Victualling with an additional £300 a year[1]. His salary as Secretary of the Admiralty was £500 a year, but he only enjoyed this for two periods amounting altogether to ten years. Yet as early as May, 1667, he was worth £6900[2]; and in the end he retired on a competence, and was able to indulge the expensive tastes of the collector. It is evident that his legitimate emoluments must have been supplemented in other ways. Readers of the *Diary* will remember that on 2 February, 1664, he received from Sir William Warren, the timber merchant, 'a pair of gloves' for his wife 'wrapt up in paper,' which he 'would not open, feeling it hard'; this phenomenon being due to the presence, presumably in the fingers, of 'forty pieces in good gold.' Warren gave him many other presents, and shewed himself 'a most useful and thankful man,'[3] bringing him on one occasion £100 'in a bag,' which Pepys 'joyfully' carried home in a coach, Warren himself 'expressly taking care that nobody might see this business

---

[1] *Diary*, 31 October, 1665.   [2] *Ib.* 31 May, 1667.
[3] *Ib.* 6 February, 1665.

done.'[1] On another occasion Captain Grove gave him money
in a paper which Pepys did not open till he reached his
office, taking the precaution of 'not looking into it till all
the money was out, that I might say I saw no money in the
paper if ever I should be questioned about it.'[2] He appears
to have profited largely by his transactions with Gauden,
the Victualler of the Navy[3]; with the Victuallers for Tangier[4]; and with Captain Cocke, a contractor for hemp[5]. He
also made profits out of flags[6], prizes[7], and Tangier freights[8];
and the *Diary* records other gifts of money and plate[9], including 'a noble silver warming-pan.'[10] On the other hand,
the official letters, numbering thousands, conspire to produce
by a series of delicate impressions the conviction in the
mind of the reader that Pepys was immensely proud of the
navy, and keenly anxious for its efficiency and success. His
attitude is affected by his fundamental Puritanism, and in
the *Diary* he is always trying to justify to himself the presents which he accepted. He was glad to do the giver a
good turn when he could, but it was with the proviso that
it should be 'without wrong to the King's service.'[11] The
inventor of such a phrase is on dangerous ground, but he is
not yet utterly debased; and the high responsibility of his
later life may very well have served as an antiseptic to arrest
corruption before it had gone far. At any rate, this is as

[1] *Diary*, 16 September, 1664.   [2] *Ib.* 3 April, 1663.
[3] *Ib.* 21 July, 1664; 4 February, 1667; 2 August, 1667.
[4] *Ib.* 16 July, 1664; 10 September, 1664; 16 March, 1665; 31 October, 1667; 27 December, 1667.
[5] *Ib.* 25 May, 27 June, 14 August, and 10 November, 1666.
[6] *Ib.* 27 November, 1664; 28 January, 1665; 28 May, 1669.
[7] *Ib.* 17 July, 1667; 14 August, 1667; 3 February, 1668.
[8] *Ib.* 28 November, 1664; 9 December, 1664; 29 March, 1665.
[9] *E.g. Ib.* 5 January, 2 May, 27 May, 3 June, 10 June, 22 June, 18 July, 21 July, 1664; 21 March, 1665; 21 February, 1668; 24 February, 1668.
[10] *Ib.* 1 January, 1669.
[11] *Ib.* 10 December, 1663. *Cf.* 5 January, 10 September, 24 September, and 12 October, 1664, where the same mental attitude is indicated.

much in advance of the cynical greed of the earlier administrators as it is behind the contempt for all forms of corruption which is natural to well-paid officials educated to
modern standards.

In 1673 the Test Act drove the Duke of York from
office, and brought about other important changes in the
administration of the navy. The King retained in his own
hands the Lord High Admiral's patronage and also the
Admiralty dues, which were to be collected for his 'only
use and behoof'; but the rest of his functions were placed
in commission[1]. There were twelve Commissioners, of whom
no less than five—the Lord Chancellor, the Lord Treasurer,
the Lord Privy Seal, and two Principal Secretaries—were
great officers of State. Prince Rupert was at the head of
the Commission, and Samuel Pepys was appointed Secretary, while the Duke of York, although no longer in office,
remained, in spite of the Test Act, an important influence
in naval affairs[2]. Pepys was succeeded in the office of Clerk
of the Acts by his brother, John Pepys, and his clerk, Thomas
Hayter, acting jointly. There were also changes in the com-
position of the Navy Board, but these did not affect its
character as a body of naval experts.

The chief business of the new administrators was to bring
to a close the Third Dutch War, and then to repair, by an
energetic shipbuilding policy, that depreciation of the navy
which was the natural result of the war. In this work they
were on the whole successful. The Admiralty Commissioners
were sensible and vigilant, and they were remarkably well
served by their Secretary; while the Navy Board was strong

---

[1] Pepysian MSS., *Miscellanies*, xi. 221, and *Calendar of State Papers,
Domestic*, 1673, p. 415.

[2] The Duke's presence 'behind the throne' is confirmed by a number of
references in the *Admiralty Letters* (*e.g.* ii. 60, 90; iii. 231, 234, 235, 301,
319, 329, 331).

on the technical side of its work, and fortunate in having as one of its members an official so thoroughly capable in his own department as the great shipbuilder, Sir Anthony Deane. Moreover, although the financial difficulty continued to hamper and cripple the navy, a vigorous shipbuilding policy was made possible by the better support which Parliament now gave to naval expansion. The idea of the importance of sea power had already acquired a considerable hold upon the political classes, and the wars with the Dutch had served to strengthen it. Charles II had read rightly the feeling of his subjects when he allowed his Chancellor to say to the Pension Parliament in the speech which opened its eleventh session: 'There is not so lawful or commendable a jealousy in the world as an Englishman's of the growing greatness of any Prince at sea.'[1] Thus the most important achievement of the period 1673–79 was the Act of 1677— the 17th century equivalent of a modern Naval Defence Act—for the building of 30 new ships. Pepys, now a member of Parliament, made in support of it a comprehensive and vigorous speech[2], and he modestly attributed the adoption of the scheme to the impression this produced upon the House. 'I doubt not,' he writes to the Navy Board, on 23 February, 1677, 'but ere this you may have heard the issue of this morning's debates in the House of Commons touching the navy, wherein I thank God the account they received from me of the past and present state thereof, compared first with one another and then with the naval force of our neighbours as it now is, different from what it ever

---

[1] Cobbett, *Parliamentary History*, iv. 587.

[2] The substance of this speech is reported in Grey's *Debates* (iv. 115), but there is in the Pepysian *Miscellanies* (ii. 453) a copy of notes for this or some other speech, entitled ' Heads for a Discourse in Parliament upon the business of the Navy, Anno 1676,' which, though it differs from the report, does not do so more widely than what an orator actually says often differs from what he intended to say. An abstract is given in *Catalogue of Pepysian MSS.*, i. 48.

heretofore has been, was so received as that the debates arising therefrom terminated in a vote for the supplying his Majesty with a sum of money for building ships.... '[1] The rates and tonnage of the 30 new ships thus provided for are specified in the Act[2].

The new programme was pushed forward with the utmost energy, but before it was completed the control of the navy again changed hands. In 1679 the excitement of the Popish Plot drove the Duke of York from England, and Pepys was involved in his disgrace. He was accused of conspiring with Sir Anthony Deane to send information about the navy to the French Government and to extirpate the Protestant religion; and was committed to the Tower on the Speaker's warrant[3]. His office at the Admiralty was, however, vacated by what was in form a voluntary resignation[4].

On the withdrawal of the Duke of York and the resignation of Pepys, the higher administration of the navy passed to a new Admiralty Commission of seven, who claimed and enjoyed, in addition to the powers of the previous Commission, those other prerogatives which the King had hitherto reserved to himself[5]. But although they had more power than their predecessors, they were much less competent to use it, for they were almost entirely without naval experience. Sir Henry Capel, the First Commissioner, had nothing to do with the navy until his appointment[6]. The same can be said of Daniel Finch, who, although he became famous afterwards

---

[1] Pepysian MSS., *Admiralty Letters*, v. 345.

[2] 29 Car. II, c. 1.

[3] *Dictionary of National Biography*, xliv. 363.

[4] Pepysian MSS., *Admiralty Letters*, ix. 282.

[5] Pepysian MSS., *Miscellanies*, ii. 411. There are two copies of their commission in the Pepysian Library (*Naval Precedents*, p. 236, and *Miscellanies*, ii. 413).

[6] *Dictionary of National Biography*, ix. 17.

as Earl of Nottingham, was at this time only a young politician just beginning his official life[1]. Sir Thomas Lee's reputation was that of a parliamentary debater[2]; and the other names are not notable. The Commission represents an intrusion of politicians into a sphere where they were quite out of place. The introduction of Lord Brouncker in 1681 was a step in the right direction, although he was not a professional seaman; and other improvements were effected in 1682, but they came too late. The Navy Board was still composed of experts, but they could not stop the mischief wrought by the incompetent authority under which they had to act. The Commissioners did not find a lenient critic in Pepys, and his comment upon them is worth quoting because it contains a shrewd appreciation of Charles II. 'No king,' he wrote in his private *Minute Book*, 'ever did so unaccountable a thing to oblige his people by, as to dissolve a Commission of the Admiralty then in his own hand, who best understands the business of the sea of any prince the world ever had, and things never better done, and put it into hands which he knew were wholly ignorant thereof, sporting himself with their ignorance.'[3] The last phrase brings before us vividly the King's characteristic way.

The result that followed was inevitable. The dockyards were disorganised; the effective force of the fleet was reduced; the reserve of stores was depleted. The Commissioners adopted a wasteful policy of retrenchment at all costs. Pepys writes of 'the effects of inexperience, daily discovering themselves' in the conduct of the Commission[4]; of 'general and habitual supineness, wastefulness, and neglect of order universally spread through' the whole navy[5], so that 'whereas peace used evermore to be improved to the

---

[1] *Dictionary of National Biography*, xix. 1.   [2] *Ib.* xxxii. 383.
[3] Pepysian MSS., No. 2866, *Naval Minutes*, p. 76.
[4] Pepys, *Memoires of the Royal Navy*, 1679–88 (Oxford reprint), p. 6.
[5] *Ib.* p. 18.

making up the wasteful effects of war, this appears…to have brought the navy into a state more deplorable in its ships and less relievable from its stores than can be shewn to have happened at the close of the most expenseful war.'[1] His indictment is supported by a formidable array of facts and figures, and as Macaulay points out[2], is confirmed by a report from an expert of the French Admiralty, so it cannot be dismissed as mere denunciation inspired by a natural prejudice against the men who had displaced him.

Things were so bad that in 1684 the Commission was revoked, and from this date until his death the office of Lord High Admiral was once more executed by the King, with the advice and assistance of 'his royal brother the Duke of York'[3]; and on his accession James II became his own Lord High Admiral. The office of Secretary of the Admiralty was revived, and Pepys was appointed thereto; and the government of the navy remained in the same hands until the Revolution.

The important episode of the period 1684–1688 is the appointment of the Special Commission of 1686 for the regeneration of the navy—an experiment in organisation for which Pepys was largely responsible[4]. A sum of £400,000 a year was to be assigned to the navy[5], and this was to be

[1] Pepys, *Memoires of the Royal Navy*, 1679–88 (Oxford reprint), p. 9.

[2] *History of England* (Longmans, 2 vols., 1880), i. 146.

[3] It is often said that the office of Lord High Admiral was restored to the Duke; but this is clearly not the view of Pepys (Pepysian MSS., *Miscellanies*, xi. 225).

[4] Materials for the history of this experiment are to be found in a manuscript volume in the Pepysian Library entitled, *My Diary relating to the Commission constituted by King James II, Anno 1686, for the Recovery of the Navy, with a Collection of the Principal Papers incident to and conclusive of the same* (Pepysian MSS., No. 1490).

[5] Pepys's ' Proposition ' is printed in his *Memoires* (pp. 18–23); and further details of the exact distribution of the £400,000 a year are given in a paper entitled 'Measures supporting my Proposition' (Pepysian MSS., No. 1490, p. 123). See also the writer's Introduction to the Oxford reprint of the *Memoires*.

administered by a body of experts, on which the two most important figures were Sir Anthony Deane, the great ship-builder, and Sir John Narbrough, the hero of the war with Algiers. The Commission was intended to last for a term of three years, the time estimated to be necessary for putting the navy into a state of thorough repair, but its work was performed with such energy and efficiency that the Commission was dissolved in October, 1688, after only $2\frac{1}{2}$ years tenure of office, and the system of government by Principal Officers and Commissioners of the Navy acting under the Lord High Admiral was restored.

The way in which Pepys manœuvred Sir Anthony Deane on to the Commission deserves a passing notice. It was not an easy matter, as Deane replied to a flattering overture by pointing out that his ordinary business as a shipwright was bringing in to him 'more than double the benefit...the common wages of a Commissioner of the Navy amounts to,' and moreover he was fifteen in family, 'and not without expectation of more.'[1] Pepys was then directed by James II to make a list of all the notable shipbuilders in England, one of whom might be selected as an alternative to Deane. The result was a very libellous and tendencious document[2]. Sir John Tippetts was dismissed because 'his age and infirmities arising from the gout (keeping him generally within doors, or at least incapable of any great action abroad) would render him wholly unable to go through the fatigue of the work designed for Sir Anthony Deane.' The second candidate, Sir Phineas Pett, is briefly dismissed with the words 'In every respect as the first.' Another candidate 'never built a ship in his life...he is also full of the gout, and by consequence as little capable as the former of the fatigue before mentioned.' Another is 'illiterate...low-spirited, of little appearance or authority'; his father 'a great drinker, and since

[1] Pepysian MSS., No. 1490, p. 131.   [2] Ib. p. 145.

3—2

killed with it.' Mr Lawrence, the master shipwright at Wool-
wich, is 'a low-spirited, slow, and gouty man...illiterate and
supine to the last degree.' Another is 'an ingenious young
man, but said rarely to have handled a tool in his life'—a mere
draughtsman. Another 'is one that loves his ease, as having
been ever used to it, not knowing what it is to work or take
pains...and very debauched.' Another is 'a good and pain-
ful, but very plain and illiterate man; a Phanatick; of no
authority and countenance.' And so he goes on through an
appalling list of disqualifications, which had their intended
effect upon the King's mind; they induced 'full conviction
of the necessity of his prevailing with and satisfying Sir A.
D.'[1] Satisfactory terms were arranged[2], and on Saturday,
13 March, 1686, Mr Pepys brought Sir Anthony Deane 'to
the King in the morning to kiss his hand, who declared the
same to him to his full satisfaction, and afterwards to my
Lord Treasurer at the Treasury Chamber with the same
mutual content.'[3]

The circumstances in which the second Secretaryship of
Samuel Pepys came to an end are part of the general history
of England, and need no repetition here. On 21 December,
1688, Pepys mentions that the King was 'a second time
withdrawn,'[4] and on Christmas Day we find him writing to
the fleet at the bidding of the Prince of Orange[5]. He continued to act as Secretary of the Admiralty until 20 February, 1689, but on 9 March he was directed to hand over his
papers to his successor, Phineas Bowles[6]. He was too inti-
mately associated with the exiled James for the government
of the Revolution to continue him in power.

---

[1] Pepysian MSS., No. 1490, p. 16.
[2] The precise nature of these does not transpire, but Deane had stated that, in
justice to his family, he could not value his whole time at less than £1000 a
year (*Ib.* p. 139). The King's first offer was £500.   [3] *Ib.* p. 17.
[4] Pepysian MSS., *Admiralty Letters*, xv. 470.   [5] *Ib.* xv. 472.
[6] *Dictionary of National Biography*, xliv. 364.

LECTURE III

FINANCE

IT is scarcely a matter for surprise that those historians who were the first to appreciate the great Puritan movement, so long under a cloud, should have yielded to the temptation of over-emphasizing the contrast between the vigour and comparative purity of government during the Interregnum and its nervelessness and corruption under the Younger Stuarts. That some such contrast exists it is impossible to deny. The Commonwealth navy was on the whole well managed, and every reader of Pepys's *Diary* knows that he was disposed to regret in private the administrative successes of the treasonable times. 3 June, 1667: 'To Spring Garden, and there eat and drank a little, and then to walk up and down the garden, reflecting upon the bad management of things now, compared with what it was in the late rebellious times, when men, some for fear and some for religion, minded their business, which none now do, by being void of both.' Or again, 4 September, 1668: 'The business of abusing the Puritans begins to grow stale and of no use, they being the people that at last will be found the wisest.' But it is possible, while dwelling upon a moral contrast, to ignore the difference in the financial situation. The virtuous Puritan colonels who controlled the navy under the Commonwealth had command of large financial resources, for confiscations and Royalist compositions were very productive, and the governments of the Interregnum could apply to the raising of taxes irresistible military force. As far as the compositions went, they were, however, living upon capital, and when this was exhausted, the pressure of financial difficulties

soon began to be felt. The maintenance of the great professional army came to be a burden too heavy for the
resources of the country as they stood in that day, and the
navy suffered from the competition of the army for the available funds. The disease usually assigned to the Restoration
period declared itself before the Restoration took place, and
when the King came back he found the navy already deep
in debt. In 1659 nearly half a million was due on account
of wages alone, and the total debt must have been over
three-quarters of a million[1]. An official report of July, 1659,
estimated the outgoings at £20,000 a week, but pointed out
that 'since May 31 has not been received above £8000 a
week.'[2] It must be remembered that with 17th century
money values these figures are very much larger than they
look, and as the State had not yet invented funding debt,
and so charging it on posterity, its position was that of an
extravagant private person. Thus the naval administrators
of the Restoration were succeeding to a bankrupt estate, and
in the *Diary* Pepys strikes a note of despair. 31 July, 1660:
the navy 'is in very sad condition, and money must be
raised for it.' 11 June, 1661: 'now the credit of the Office
is brought so low, that none will sell us anything without
our personal security given for the same.' 31 August, 1661:
'we are at our Office quiet, only for lack of money all things
go to rack.' 30 September, 1661: 'the want of money puts
all things, and above all the Navy, out of order.' 28 June,
1662: 'God knows, the King is not able to set out five ships
at this present without great difficulty, we neither having
money, credit, nor stores.'

The same difficulties were felt before, during, and after the
Second Dutch War. In September, 1664, when war was impending, Commissioner Pett tried to buy tallow and candles
for the navy at Maidstone, but found the country 'so shy'

---

[1] A. W. Tedder, *The Navy of the Restoration*, p. 41.   [2] *Ib.* p. 41 *n.*

that they refused to deal[1]. In January, 1666, the Commissioner at Portsmouth wrote that all men distrust London pay[2]. Nearly half the letters to the Navy Board calendared for 1665–6 refer to the difficulties experienced by government agents in obtaining supplies[3]. In this way bargains were lost for want of ready money[4], and where credit was obtained, enormous prices had to be paid[5]. The hardships to private persons were intolerable. A firm of slop-sellers who had supplied goods to the value of £24,800 during the last two years, and had received only £800, would shortly be ruined in their estates and families[6]. A Bristol shipbuilder writes: 'I have so disabled myself in the relief of poor workmen that I am now out of a capacity of relieving mine own family: I have disbursed and engaged for more than I am worth.'[7] The Barber Surgeons' Company claim £1,496. 6s. 10d., long unpaid, for filling medicine chests, and complain of the opprobrious language they receive from surgeons who can get no pay[8]; and a certain poor widow, a creditor of the government, is in a most deplorable condition, without a stick of wood or coals to lay on the fire, and owing money to about fifteen people as poor as herself, who torment her daily[9].

The total annual charge of the navy in time of peace is not easy to calculate. On 18 February, 1663[10], Pepys him-

[1] *State Papers, Domestic, Charles II*, cii. 123.

[2] *Calendar of State Papers, Domestic*, 1665–6, p. 189. See also *ib.* 1666–7, p. 233, and *Diary*, 20 June, 1667.

[3] *Ib.* 1665–6, p. xxxix.   [4] *Ib.* 1666–7, p. 228, and 1665–6, p. 189.

[5] Even in 1658 the Navy Commissioners had been obliged to buy at from 30 to 50 per cent. above the market price (M. Oppenheim, *The Administration of the Royal Navy*, 1509–1660, p. 351).

[6] *Calendar of State Papers, Domestic*, 1664–5, p. 353.

[7] *State Papers, Domestic, Charles II*, ccxlii. 56; *Calendar of State Papers, Domestic*, 1667–8, p. 563.

[8] *Calendar of State Papers, Domestic*, 1667, p. 454.

[9] *Cf. ib.* 1667–8, p. 455 and 1666–7, p. 233.

[10] *Diary*.

self estimated 'the true charge of the Navy,' since the King's
coming in to Christmas last, to have been 'after the rate of
£374,743 a year,' but it is not clear what this figure includes.
Perhaps the pre-war expenditure may be put at not far
short of £400,000. In a letter to Sir Philip Warwick, dated
14 March, 1666[1], he supplies materials for estimating expenditure in time of war. So enormous were the arrears that
the sum of £2,312,876 would be needed to pay the fleet and
yards to 1 August, 1665, to clear off the arrears of the Victualler and provide victuals for the current year, to finish
ten new ships that had been ordered, and to meet wear
and tear and wages for the first ten months of 1666. Towards this the total funds available, including a Parliamentary grant of £1,250,000 made in October, 1665, amounted
to £1,498,483. Thus there was a deficit of £814,393. But
to this would have to be added other charges not included
in the first estimate—principally wear and tear and wages
for the last two months of 1666, arrears of wages, and other
debts, which would increase the deficit to £1,277,161, over
and above 'the whole expense of the Office of the Ordnance.' In other words, the funds available for the navy in
March, 1666, in the second year of the war, were scarcely
more than half its probable requirements[2]. Nevertheless,
Pepys derived great consolation from a calculation which
he had made of the cost of the First Dutch War in 1653,
whereby it appeared that 'the State's charge then seems to
have exceeded the King's for the same service and time by
£171,785.'[3] This is the justification of a note in the *Diary*

[1] Pepysian MSS., No. 2589, pp. 1–3.
[2] Another statement of the expenditure of the navy during the Second Dutch
War is to be found in a letter from the Navy Board to the Lord Treasurer,
dated 24 September, 1666, which gives for the information of Parliament, just
then about to meet, an estimate for the period 1 September, 1664, to 29 September,
1666. This calculation is given in the writer's *Catalogue of Pepysian MSS.*, i. 102.
[3] Pepysian MSS., No. 2589, p. 118.

of 16 March, 1669: 'Upon the whole do find that the late times in all their management were not more husbandly than we.' To meet the situation recourse was again had to Parliament, and in October, 1666, the Commons voted £1,800,000, although their suspicion that the money was being wasted led to the appointment of that Commission of Public Accounts which was to give Pepys and his colleagues infinite trouble[1], and was to lay the foundation of Parliamentary enquiry into the proceedings of the executive.

As soon as the war came to an end, the higher authorities began to consider schemes of retrenchment in the navy. A committee appointed 29 July, 1667, by Order in Council, to consider the King's expenses called for a report upon the cost of the navy, and the Duke of York put forward some preliminary suggestions[2], the most important being a reduction of certain establishments and the closing of the dockyard at Harwich. He also suggested a reduction in the number of the Commissioners from ten to six, or at most seven, although he was disposed to resist any great reduction in their salaries on the ground that these should be sufficient to make the Principal Officers and Commissioners 'value their employments, and not subject them to a necessity of base compliances with others to the King's prejudice, by which to get one shilling to himself he must lose ten to the King, and when he shall have once subjected himself to an inferior pleasure by such a falsehood, he never more dares act the part of a good officer, being by his former guilt become a slave to his inferior.' This argument, while it served incidentally to protect Pepys's emoluments, is not a bad statement of the case for a living wage as an antidote to corruption. The scheme eventually adopted, suggested by Sir William Coventry, aimed at a reduction of peace

[1] Ranke, *History of England*, iii. 449–50; see also the *Diary*.
[2] *State Papers, Domestic, Charles II*, ccxiii. 65.

expenditure to £200,000 a year[1], but the goal was never
reached, for the naval expenditure of the next two or three
years was not, as a matter of fact, limited to the £200,000
a year proposed, nor was ready money provided—an essential condition of the scheme. The policy of retrenchment
on a great scale would have to be carried on for a long time
before it could affect the accumulated masses of the navy
debt[2], and there is abundant evidence of continued financial
stringency after the war as well as before it. This carried
its nemesis into the Third Dutch War. The comparative
failure of the naval operations of 1673 was due to the fact
that the fleet had been sent out insufficiently manned and
equipped; and the want of a reserve of stores and of men
and materials for refitting occasioned the loss of nearly six
weeks in the best season of the year[3].

As soon as the Third Dutch War came to an end in
February, 1674, another period of feverish retrenchment
set in, and an attempt was made 'to lessen the growing
charge in the navy, towards which no one particular seems
more to conduce than that of reducing the number of the
persons employed therein, both at sea and in the yards.'[4]
Other economies were also practised. Ships as they came
in were paid off and laid up[5], and it was decided to under-
take no new works 'until his Majesty hath in some measure

[1] Penn, *Memorials of Sir William Penn*, ii. 528; *Calendar of State Papers,
Domestic*, 1667, p. 420. On Coventry's connexion with the scheme see *Diary*,
19 August, 1667. Particulars of it are given in *Catalogue of Pepysian MSS.*,
i. 104. With this calculation should be compared a detailed estimate of the
annual charge of 'his Maesty's navy in harbour' for the year 1684 (Pepysian
MSS., No. 2867, *Naval Precedents*, p. 402), the substance of which is given
in *Catalogue of Pepysian MSS.*, i. 111. The total is £135,084. 6s. 11d., but
this is exclusive of ships at sea.

[2] Estimated at the end of the war as £1,100,000 (*Calendar of State Papers,
Domestic*, 1667, p. 471).

[3] *Calendar of State Papers, Domestic*, 1673, pp. x, 218, 333, 341, 510.

[4] Pepysian MSS., *Admiralty Letters*, iii. 130.   [5] *Ib.* iii. 182.

got over the debt which remains to him upon the old.'[1] Meanwhile the official correspondence contains frequent references to the shortness of money. For instance, in January, 1674, the *Swan* was delayed at Plymouth 'from the unwillingness of the tradesmen to trust his Majesty further'[2]; and in December, 1677, Pepys reports from Sir John Kempthorne that 'the brewer at Portsmouth doth absolutely declare that he will not provide any beer for the *Rupert* and *Centurion* till he is better assured of his payment than he now is.'[3] At the beginning of 1678 the situation was somewhat relieved by the Parliamentary vote for preparations against France, but this improvement was of short duration, and in December we find Pepys referring to one of the most wasteful consequences of a want of money—'that mighty charge which has so long lain upon our hands for want of money wherewith to discharge those of the ships which remain yet unpaid off.'[4]

In spite of the frequent references to want of funds scattered up and down the official correspondence, the financial position of the navy greatly improved in the later years of the Restoration period. At Lady Day, 1686, the debts of the Navy Office were reckoned at £171,836. 2s. 9d.—a remarkable reduction on the enormous totals of 1666[5]. After the accession of James II no less than £305,806 was paid by the Treasurer of the Navy on account of debts incurred in Charles II's reign[6], so it is not surprising to find that,

[1] Pepysian MSS., *Admiralty Letters*, iii. 186.

[2] *Ib.* iii. 49, 51, 52.

[3] *Ib.* vi. 277. Other instances are given in *Catalogue of Pepysian MSS.*, i. 108.

[4] *Ib.* viii. 403.

[5] *A State of the Debt contracted in the Navy between* 1 *January*, 1671[–2]... *and* 25 *March*, 1686, *and which remains at this day unpaid according to the books in this Office...* (Pepysian MSS., *Miscellanies*, xi. 18). This paper is printed in *Catalogue of Pepysian MSS.*, i. 110.

[6] Pepysian MSS., *Miscellanies*, xi. 20.

both in the closing years of Charles II and the earlier years
of James II, money was still difficult to get, and the old
complaints recur although in a less aggravated form.

Bearing in mind these facts about finance, let us pass on
to consider some of their practical results.

During the period from 1660 to 1688 the operations of
the navy were grievously hampered by the deficiency of
men, both in the dockyards and at sea; and this deficiency
was mainly, if not entirely, due to the want of pay.

The state of things during the Second Dutch War was
appalling. The *Diary* contains pitiable stories of poor seamen starving in the streets because there was no money to
pay their wages. 7 October, 1665: 'Did business, though
not much, at the Office; because of the horrible crowd and
lamentable moan of the poor seamen that lie starving in
the streets for lack of money, which do trouble and per-
plex me to the heart; and more at noon when we were to
go through them, for then a whole hundred of them followed
us; some cursing, some swearing, and some praying to us.'[1]
We hear of wages nine months[2], twenty-two[3], twenty-six,
thirty-four[4], and even fifty-two[5] months in arrear. One
captain with a breezy style complains that for want of
pay 'instead of a young commander, he is rendered an old
beggar.'[6] The crews of two ships petition the Navy Board
to order them their pay 'that their families may not be
altogether starved in the streets, and themselves go like
heathens, having nothing to cover their nakedness.'[7] The
Commissioner at Portsmouth writes of workmen in the yard

---

[1] *Cf. Diary*, 6 July, 1665, 30 September, 1665, 31 October, 1665, and
12 March, 1667.

[2] *Calendar of State Papers, Domestic*, 1664–5, p. 304.

[3] *Ib* 1667, p. 46.   [4] *Ib.* 1667, p. 75.

[5] *Ib.* 1667, p. lx note. See also p. 514.   [6] *Ib.* 1665–6, p. 385.

[7] *Ib.* 1667, p. lx note, and p. 514.

there, that they are turned out of doors by their landlords, and perish more like dogs than men[1].

Naturally enough, this state of things affected discipline. The crews of the *Little Victory* and the *Pearl* at Hull mutinied for want of pay, and refused to weigh anchor[2], and in the yards the workmen gave a great deal of trouble. The Chatham shipwrights and caulkers, to whom two years' wages were owing, marched up to London to appeal to the Navy Board, as 'their families are denied trust and cannot subsist,' and under this pressure we are told that arrangements were made 'to pay off some of the most disorderly.'[3] At Chatham the Commissioner writes that he is almost torn to pieces by the workmen of the yard for their weekly pay[4]. Sir John Mennes writes from Portsmouth on 14 July, 1665, for money to be sent immediately to stop 'the bawlings and impatience of these people, especially of their wives, whose tongues are as foul as the daughters of Billingsgate.'[5] Apparently the money did not come, and in October the Commissioner was forced to lend the men ten shillings apiece to keep them from mutiny[6]. A fortnight later a mutiny actually broke out, but Commissioner Middleton shewed praiseworthy promptitude in dealing with it. According to his own account, he seized 'a good cudgel' out of the hands of one of the men, and took more pains in the use of it than in any business for the last twelve months. He adds: 'I have not been troubled since.'[7] On 27 October, 1666, the outlook in London was so threatening that the Navy Board applied to the Officers of the Ordnance for 'twelve well-fixed firelocks with a supply of powder and bullet' for the defence of the Navy Office, in view of 'the

[1] *Calendar of State Papers, Domestic,* 1664–5, p. 522.
[2] *Ib.* 1667, p. 75. [3] *Ib.* 1667–8, p. xiv.
[4] *Ib.* 1667–8, p. 443. [5] *Ib.* 1664–5, p. 475.
[6] *Ib.* 1665–6, p. 32. [7] *Ib.* 1665–6, p. 53.

present great refractoriness and tumultuousness of the sea-men.'[1] Nor did the trouble end when peace came, for the financial situation was still difficult. On 11 March, 1671, Jonas Shish wrote from Deptford to the Navy Board: 'The shipwrights and caulkers are very much enraged by reason that their wages is not paid them. The last night the whole street next the King's Yard, both of men and women, was in an uproar, and meeting with Mr Bagwell, my fore-man, they fell on him, and it was God's great mercy they had not spoiled him. I was then without the gate at my son's house, and hearing the tumult, I did think how Israel stoned Hadoram that was over the tribute, and King Reho-boam made speed and gat him up to fly to Jerusalem, so I gat speedily into the King's Yard, for I judge if the rude multitude had met with me, I should have had worse measure than my foreman.'[2]

In view of these facts about pay, it is not surprising that it was found difficult to obtain men. In order to man the fleets for service against the Dutch it was necessary to employ the press, and this produced very poor material. Pepys notes in 1666 that men were pressed in London that 'were not liable to it,' 'poor patient labouring men and housekeepers,'[3] and he adds 'it is a great tyranny.' The redoubtable Commissioner Middleton, writing from Ports-mouth on 29 March, 1666, tells Pepys that he is ashamed to see such pressed men as are sent from Devonshire—one with the falling sickness and a lame arm; another with dead palsy on one side and not any use of his right arm[4]. A year later he makes similar complaints from Chatham with regard to the pressed men supplied by Watermen's Hall. 'The

---

[1] Historical MSS. Commission, *Fifteenth Report*, Appendix, pt. ii., p. 167.
[2] *State Papers, Domestic, Charles II*, ccxcvii. 19. Other instances are given in *Catalogue of Pepysian MSS.*, i. 120.
[3] *Diary*, 1 and 2 July, 1666.
[4] *Calendar of State Papers, Domestic*, 1665–6, p. 323.

Masters of Watermen's Hall are good Christians but very knaves; they should be ordered to send down ten or twelve old women to be nurses to the children they send.'[1]

On the outbreak of the Third Dutch War in 1672 the same difficulties recurred, but the complaints are less frequent and less serious, and the condition of things had evidently improved. But ships had still to be manned by pressing, and the quality of the pressed men left much to be desired. For instance, two watermen, pressed in 1673, are described as 'little children, and never at sea before,' who could not be suffered 'to pester the ship.'[2]

'It can never be well in the navy,' wrote Pepys on 5 September, 1680, 'till the poor seamen can be paid once in a year at furthest, and tickets answered like bills of exchange; whereas at this very day...ships are kept out two or three years, and four of them just now ordered forth again only for want of money, after being brought in to be paid off.'[3] A little later he notes the effect of this upon discipline[4], and comments on the 'unreasonable hardship' entailed by 'the general practice of our navy' 'of paying those ships off first where the least sum clears the most men; those who have served longest, and therefore need their pay most, being postponed to those who have served least.'[5] In a maturer reflection made after his retirement, dated December, 1692,

---

[1] *Calendar of State Papers, Domestic,* 1667–8, p. xv. As late as 1742 Captain John Hamilton reports the pressing of a lime-burner who was nearly blind, and 'a little old cobbler of 56, taken out of his stall rather it should seem for a pastime than service'; and letters of 1747 shew that the pressing of mere lads, or of persons not able-bodied, was a subject of 'general and constant complaint' (Public Record Office, *Captains' Letters,* H 12; *Secretary's Letters,* 3). In 1864 or 1865 a 'man' who weighed 70 lbs. was sent on board the *Prince Consort* at Spithead.

[2] 13 April, 1673: *State Papers, Domestic, Charles II,* cccxliii. 141. See also *Calendar of State Papers, Domestic,* 1673, p. 228.

[3] Pepysian MSS., No. 2866, *Naval Minutes,* p. 24.

[4] *Ib.* p. 39.   [5] *Ib.* p. 71.

Pepys still places the 'length and badness of the payment
of the seaman's wages' first among his 'discouragements.'
This, together with 'their ill-usage from commanders, and
want of permission to help themselves in intervals of public
service by a temporary liberty of earning a penny in the
merchant's' are 'discouragements that I cannot think anything can be proposed of temptations of other kinds sufficient
to reconcile them to.'[1] Nevertheless, Pepys claimed credit
for more punctual payments for the Special Commission of
1686, during the time they held office. 'Not a penny left unpaid,' he writes, 'to any officer, seaman, workman, artificer,
or merchant, for any service done in, or commodity delivered
to the use of the Navy, either at sea or on shore, within the
whole time of this Commission, where the party claiming
the same was in the way to receive it.'[2]

In connexion with the seamen something should be said
about the organisation for the care of the sick and wounded.
The credit of being the first English Government to recog-
nise the obligation of providing for the sick and wounded
belongs to the Commonwealth. The principle that the State
should provide for those who had suffered in its service was
laid down by the Long Parliament in 1642, and an attempt
was made to apply it to the case of soldiers wounded in the
Civil War[3]. A little later the same principle was applied to
seamen, and the idea and the machinery were taken over by
the Restoration statesmen. In October, 1664, in view of the
impending war with the Dutch, a temporary Commission
for the care of Sick and Wounded Seamen on the model of
the Commission of 1653 was appointed for the duration of
the war, the most active member of it being John Evelyn,

---

[1] Pepysian MSS., No. 2866, *Naval Minutes*, p. 287.
[2] *Memoires of the Royal Navy* (Oxford reprint), p. 80.
[3] C. H. Firth, *Cromwell's Army*, ch. ix.

the diarist[1]. This Commission was re-appointed in March, 1672, for the Third Dutch War, and the elaborate instructions given to it are to be found in the volume of *Naval Precedents* in the Pepysian Library[2]. The Commissioners were to distribute the sick and wounded among the hospitals of England, 'thereby to ease his Majesty's charge'; and as soon as this accommodation was exhausted, they were to billet them upon private persons at the King's expense. London, Yarmouth, Ipswich, Southwold, Aldeburgh, Harwich, Chatham, Gravesend, Deal, Dover, Gosport, Southampton, Weymouth, Dartmouth, and Plymouth were specially assigned for the reception of sick and wounded men set ashore from their ships. At these 'places of reception' as they were called, the Commissioners were to appoint an agent, and to provide 'a physician (if need be) and chirurgeon, and nurses, fire, candle, linen, medicaments, and all things necessary,' but in ' as husbandly and thrifty a manner' as might be. The Commission was also charged with the care of prisoners of war, and was instructed to provide for their maintenance on a scale 'not exceeding 5d. per diem for every common seaman and inferior officer, and 12d. per diem for every commission officer.' For a time also it was concerned with awarding gratuities to the 'widows, children, and impotent parents of such as shall be slain in his Majesty's service at sea'; but in 1673 these duties were taken over by another commission, for Widows and Orphans, and a regular scale was established on which gratuities were to be given. Widows of men slain in the service were to receive a gratuity equal to eleven months of their husband's pay, an additional third being allowed to each orphan except those who were married at the time of the father's death. If the deceased left no widow, his mother was to receive the

[1] Evelyn's *Diary* (ed. Austin Dobson), ii. 218.
[2] Pepysian MSS., No. 2867, pp. 537-53.

T.   4

bounty, provided that she was herself a widow, indigent, and over 50 years of age. The bounty to a child was to be allowed to accumulate until it was of an age to be apprenticed. This Commission terminated at the end of the war, and by an order of 21 December, 1674, its functions devolved on the Navy Board.

These arrangements were all admirable upon paper, and the members of the Commissions displayed indefatigable industry, but in this department of affairs as in others the best of schemes were wrecked on the rock of finance. On 30 September, 1665, Evelyn wrote that he had 5000 sick, wounded, and prisoners dying for want of bread and shelter. 'His Majesty's subjects,' he adds, 'die in our sight and at our thresholds without our being able to relieve them, which, with our barbarous exposure of the prisoners to the utmost of sufferings, must needs redound to his Majesty's great dishonour, and to the consequence of losing the hearts of our own people, who are ready to execrate and stone us as we pass.'[1] On 5 June, 1672, the same loyal and humane gentleman wrote in a similar strain from Rochester: 'I have near 600 sick and wounded men in this place, 200 prisoners, and the apprehension of hundreds more....I hope there will be care to supply my district here with moneys, or else I shall be very miserable, for no poor creature does earn his bread with greater anxiety than I at present.'[2] The moneys did not come, and by the end of the summer some of the localities were becoming restive at the non-payment of arrears. There was a great deal of noise made at Gravesend when the Commissioners of the Navy passed by, and on 27 August Evelyn wrote to Pepys: 'Those cursed people of Gravesend have no bowels, and swear that they will receive not a man

---

[1] *State Papers, Domestic, Charles II,* cxxxiii. 63; see also *Calendar of State Papers, Domestic,* 1666–7, p. 398.
[2] *Calendar of State Papers, Domestic,* 1672, p. 157.

more till their arrears are discharged. We are above £2000 indebted in Kent, where our daily charge is £100 for quarters only. Judge by this how comfortable a station I am in.'[1]

When the war came to an end the temporary Commission was withdrawn, and by a warrant from the Lords of the Admiralty dated 28 March, 1674, its duties were handed over to James Pearse, 'chirurgeon-general of his Majesty's navy.'[2] Pearse was a man of business after Pepys's own heart, and he carefully systematised the whole of his functions, reducing them 'into such a method that it is not possible for me (or whomsoever shall succeed me) to wrong his Majesty or injure his subjects.'[3]

'Mariners and soldiers maimed in his Majesty's service at sea' were entitled to relief out of the Chest at Chatham, a fund provided by deducting 6d. a month from each man's pay. Fourpence a month was also deducted for the maintenance of a chaplain, and Pepys explains how the Chest benefited from an arrangement by which all moneys were also assigned to it 'arising out of the seamen's contributions for a chaplain upon ships where (by the remissness or impiety of the commander) no chaplain is provided.'[4] A paper of 24 July, 1685[5], gives the scale of this relief:

A leg or arm lost is £6. 13. 4. paid as present relief, and
    so much settled as an annual pension for his life-
    time £6 13 4
If two legs be lost his pension is doubled   .   .   . £13 6 8

---

[1] *State Papers, Domestic, Charles II*, cccxxviii. 114.

[2] Pepysian MSS., *Miscellanies*, xi. 106.

[3] *Ib.* xi. pp. 103–110, where Pearse's report of September, 1687, giving an account of the reforms effected by him during his long tenure of office, is pasted into the volume. The substance of this is printed in *Catalogue of Pepysian MSS.*, i. 137.

[4] *Catalogue of Pepysian MSS.*, i. 205.

[5] Pepysian MSS., *Miscellanies*, vi. 71.

For the loss of two arms, in consideration of his being
    thereby rendered uncapable of getting a livelihood
    any other way, per annum £15 0 0
But if an arm be on, and disabled only, is £5 per annum £5 0 0
An eye lost is £4 per annum £4 0 0
...And where any wound or hurt occasions a fracture, contusion, im-
postumation, or the like, under the loss of a limb, such are viewed by
the chirurgeons, and certified to deserve what in their opinions may be
a proportionable reward in full satisfaction. And these sorts of hurts
frequently accompany the loss of a limb in other parts of the body, for
which they have a reward apart from their annual allowance, according
to the chirurgeon's discretion.

One more question remains for our consideration to-day—
that of the rates of pay in the navy during the period 1660–88.

As far as the rates themselves were concerned the story
is one of steady improvement. In 1653 the pay of a general
or admiral of the fleet had been £3 a day during his employment; of a vice-admiral, £2; and of a rear-admiral, £1[1].
The scale adopted by Order in Council, 26 February, 1666[2],
raised the admiral's pay from £3 to £4; the vice-admiral's
from £2 to £2. 10s.; and the rear-admiral's from £1 to £2.
The vice-admiral of a squadron only was to get 30s. and the
rear-admiral of a squadron £1. The pay of the other officers
was not increased beyond the rates fixed in 1653[3]. The able
seamen in 1660 received 24s. a month; the ordinary seamen,
19s.; the apprentices or 'gromets,' 14s. 3d.; and the 'boys,'
9s. 6d. The wages of the carpenter, boatswain, and gunner
varied from £2 to £4 a month according to the rate of the
ship. Monthly wages in harbour, as distinguished from sea
wages, were on a lower scale[4]. In 1686 a new establishment

[1] *State Papers, Domestic, Interr.* xxxii. 39.
[2] Pepysian MSS., No. 2867, *Naval Precedents*, p. 217.
[3] A table of these rates is given in Oppenheim, p. 360.
[4] See Pepysian MSS., No. 488, *King James II's Pocket Book of Rates and
Memorandums.* Tables of harbour and rigging wages taken from this source
are printed in *Catalogue of Pepysian MSS.,* i. 141.

of wages[1] made a few minor changes, but the pay of the seamen was not affected thereby.

The misfortune of the 'poor seaman' was not that his rate of pay was insufficient, but that he could not get his money, or if he got it at all it was in the depreciated paper currency known as the 'ticket.' A ticket was a certificate from the officers of his ship, issued to each seaman, specifying the term and quality of his service. This, when countersigned by the Navy Board, was the seaman's warrant for demanding his wages from the Treasurer of the Navy on shore. The original purpose of tickets was to save the necessity of transporting large sums of money on board ship, but the want of funds in the navy soon made it the regular practice to treat tickets as inconvertible paper, and to discharge all seamen with tickets instead of money—or with money for part of their time and a ticket for the rest. Theoretically, the ticket should have supplied the seaman with credit almost up to the full amount of his wages, but in practice the long waiting and uncertainty of payment caused a great depreciation of tickets. We hear of women brokers standing about the Navy Office, offering to help seamen who might have tickets to ready money—but always upon terms. They took them to Mrs Salesbury in Carpenter's Yard, near Aldgate, who bought them for cash at a discount of at least 5s. in the £, and sometimes more[2]. This caused great discontent among the seamen, who naturally objected to being paid by the State in depreciated paper, and on 13 February, 1667, Pepys records in the *Diary* that 'there was a very great disorder this day at the Ticket Office, to the beating and bruising of the face' of one Car-

---

[1] Pepysian MSS., No. 2867, *Naval Precedents*, pp. 195–6. This new table of wages is printed in *Catalogue of Pepysian MSS.*, i. 150.

[2] *Catalogue of State Papers, Domestic*, 1666–7, p. 426; see also *ib.* 1665–6, p. 75.

casse, the clerk. The grievance attracted attention, and in
1667 the House of Commons enquired into 'the buying and
selling of tickets.'[1] The 'infinite great disorder' of the Ticket
Office also attracted the notice of the Commissioners of
Public Accounts[2], but the reply of the Navy Board when
invited to justify the practice was conclusive. 'We conceive
the use of tickets to be by no other means removable than
by a supply of money in every place, at all times, in readiness
where and when...any...occasions of discharging seamen
shall arise.'[3]

Apart from the disastrous results of the practice of issuing
tickets without money to pay them, the actual machinery of
the system was better under Charles II than it had hitherto
been. Printed tickets with counterfoils had been invented
under the Commonwealth, and were in use as early as August,
1654[4]; but in 1667 elaborate instructions for the examining
and signing of tickets and comparing them with the counterfoils were issued by the Navy Board to protect the Office
against fraud[5]. John Hollond complains of the abuses to
which even a solvent ticket system gave rise. It enabled
'wrong parties' to secure the seaman's wages—these being
'such as have wrought upon the advantage of the men's
necessities'—'either pursers, clerks of the check, or creditors,
whether alehouse-keepers, or slopsellers, or else pretended
sweethearts.'[6] He also notes the facilities which the system
afforded for the abuse of 'dead pays,' tickets being issued
for seamen who were dead or who never served, and men
suborned to personate them at the pay-table[7]. This was
particularly easy in time of war, when the pressure of

[1] *Diary*, 13 November, 1667.
[2] Pepysian MSS., *Miscellanies*, vi. 465–80.
[3] Penn, *Memorials of Sir William Penn*, ii. 509.
[4] *Calendar of State Papers, Domestic*, 1654, p. 548.
[5] Pepysian MSS., No. 2554.
[6] *Discourses*, p. 129 and *nn*.   [7] *Ib.* p. 140.

business was too great to allow of the tickets being properly examined.

A new and important principle in connexion with the pay of naval officers was established in 1668. Deane had urged in 1653 that seamen should be entered for continuous service and kept on continuous pay like soldiers[1], but the practice of the navy was quite different, both for officers and men. Hitherto it had been usual to regard naval officers as appointed for particular services, and possessing no claim upon the Government when these services had been discharged. The result of this was that, except in time of war, the field of employment was far too small, and a number of good officers were thrown upon their own resources. But at the close of the Second Dutch War the Government formally recognised for the first time the claims of officers to pay in time of peace. The first step did not go far, but the principle now accepted was destined to lead to the modern system of continuous employment. By an Order in Council of 17 July, 1668[2], it was provided that, in consideration of 'the eminent services performed in the late war against the Dutch by the flag officers,' and the fact that 'during the time of peace several of them are out of employment, and thereby disabled to support themselves in a condition answerable to their merits and those marks of honour his Majesty hath conferred on them,' they should receive ' pensions ' in proportion to the scale of pay on active service which had been fixed at the beginning of the war. These ' pensions ' ranged from £150 a year for captains of flag-ships up to £250 a year for rear-admirals and vice-admirals of fleets[3]. By an Order of 26 June, 1674, the same scale was established for flag officers who

---

[1] *Dictionary of National Biography*, xiv. 257.

[2] Pepysian MSS., No. 2867, *Naval Precedents*, p. 477. There is a reference to this in the *Diary*, 6.July, 1668. Sir William Coventry was against it, and Pepys agreed with him.

[3] The scale is given in *Catalogue of Pepysian MSS.*, i. 145

had served in the Third Dutch War[1]; and in 1674 and 1675 the system of half-pay for officers when they were not being actually employed was further extended to the captains and masters of first and second rate ships who had served in the war[2], and to the commanders of squadrons[3].

In 1672[4] another important change relating to pay was made by the Council. The principle of pensions on superannuation was adopted for officers. These were to be 'equal to the salary and known allowances they enjoyed,' provided that they had completed fifteen years of service 'where the employment is constant, such as that of boatswains, gunners, pursers, carpenters, &c.,' or eight years where it is not constant, 'such as that of masters, chirurgeons, &c.' In 1673[5] the principle of superannuation was extended from cases of old age to officers wounded in service at sea. Such officers were to receive one year's wages, 'and the continuance of them in pay during the whole time they shall by good proof appear to have lain under cure.'

---

[1] *Naval Precedents*, p. 222.

[2] Order in Council of 6 May, 1674 (*Naval Precedents*, p. 164; see also p. 259). The substance of the Order is given in *Catalogue of Pepysian MSS.*, i. 146.

[3] Order in Council, 19 May, 1675 (*Naval Precedents*, p. 165). The substance of the Order is given in *Catalogue of Pepysian MSS.*, i. 147.

[4] Order in Council, 6 December, 1672 (*Naval Precedents*, p. 198).

[5] Order in Council, 6 June, 1673 (*Naval Precedents*, p. 218). There is another copy in *Miscellanies*, vi. 67. For subsequent extensions of the Order, in 1673 and 1674, see *Catalogue of Pepysian MSS.*, i. 148-9.

LECTURE IV

VICTUALLING; DISCIPLINE; SHIPS; GUNS

THE arrangements for victualling had always had an important bearing upon the contentment and efficiency of the seamen. 'However the pay of the mariners, both for sea and harbour, may be wanting for some time,' wrote one of the Victuallers, 'yet they must have continual supplies of victuals, otherwise they will be apt to fall into very great disorders.'[1] Pepys, in his private *Minute Book*[2], makes the same point. 'Englishmen,' he says, 'and more especially seamen, love their bellies above anything else, and therefore it must always be remembered, in the management of the victualling of the navy, that to make any abatement from them in the quantity or agreeableness of the victuals, is to discourage and provoke them in the tenderest point, and will sooner render them disgusted with the King's service than any one other hardship that can be put upon them.' But in this department also the want of money had fatal effects, and contributed more than any other cause to the comparative failure of the administration to provide victuals of good quality, sufficient quantity, and promptly delivered where they were required.

Before the Restoration the victualling was being managed by Victualling Commissioners 'upon account,' the State keeping the business in its own hands[3]. But the system had scarcely a fair trial owing to financial embarrassments[4],

---

[1] *State Papers, Domestic, Charles II*, ccxcix. 121.
[2] P. 254.
[3] Hollond, *Discourses*, pp. 124, 154.
[4] Oppenheim, p. 326.

and just before the King's return matters were as bad as they could well be[1]. The restored Government reverted to the older system of contract, and in September, 1660, Denis Gauden was appointed contractor under the satisfying title of 'surveyor-general of all victuals to be provided for his Majesty's ships and maritime causes,' with a fee of £50 a year, and 8d. a day for a clerk[2]. The whole burden of the victualling therefore rested upon a single man, and when the war with the Dutch broke out, he was unable to grapple with its demands; yet no fundamental change could be made in the system until the Government was in a position to settle accounts with him. Thus the victuals, although on the whole good in quality, were deficient in quantity, and when Gauden was remonstrated with he could always reply, and generally with perfect truth, that it was impossible for him to do better as long as the Government failed to carry out their part of the contract, and to make payments on account at the stipulated times[3]. In the spring of 1665, when the fleet was fitting for sea, complaints of the failure of the Victualler were frequent[4]. Later on, when Pepys went down to visit the fleet in September, Lord Sandwich told him that most of the ships had been without beer 'these three weeks or month, and but few days' dry provisions.'[5] In this year complaints of uneatable provisions occur, though not often, but when they were bad they were sometimes very bad. On 10 August, Commissioner Middleton wrote to Pepys from Portsmouth that the *Coventry* was still in port; her beer had nearly poisoned one man, who 'being thirsty drank a

[1] Oppenheim, p. 327.
[2] *State Papers, Domestic, Charles II*, Docquet Book, p. 46.
[3] *Calendar of State Papers, Domestic*, 1665-6, p. xxxix. See also pp. 23, 27, 55, 203.
[4] *Ib.* 1664-5, pp. 306, 311, 317, 321, 382.
[5] *Diary*, 18 September, 1665.

great draught.'[1] Probably now, as undoubtedly later, the backwardness of the victualling in turn reacted upon the deficiency of men, for the sailors deserted from ships where they could get no food[2].

The practical breakdown of the victualling system during the spring and summer of 1665 led to the establishment, at Pepys's suggestion, of new machinery for keeping the Victualler up to the mark—a Surveyor of Victuals appointed at the King's charge in each port, with power to examine the Victualler's books; and a central officer in London to whom they were to report weekly[3]. As soon as Pepys's plan was adopted, he wrote to suggest that he himself should be the new Surveyor-General of Victualling[4], and on 27 October he accepted office[5] at a salary of £300 a year[6]. The appointment was temporary only, and came to an end at the conclusion of peace. While it lasted it effected a slight improvement. Pepys himself was much pleased with the success of his arrangements, and he was complimented upon them by the Duke of York[7]. As he had £500 a year from Gauden as well as the £300 from the King[8], he managed to do well out of the war.

The experience of the war had shewn the weak points of the one-man system, and in subsequent contracts several Victuallers were associated in a kind of partnership[9], but the fundamental difficulty was one of finance, and this a mere multiplication of persons did little to meet. Thus there are complaints in 1671[10], and the difficulties were greatly

[1] *State Papers, Domestic, Charles II*, cxxviii. 85; see also *Calendar of State Papers, Domestic*, 1664–5, p. 480.

[2] *Calendar of State Papers, Domestic*, 1667–8, p. xviii.

[3] *Ib.* 1665–6, p. 7; see also p. 11, and *Diary*, 14 October, 1665.

[4] *Diary*, 19 October, 1665.

[5] *Ib.* 27 October, 1665.

[6] *Ib.* 31 October, 1665.

[7] *Ib.* 26 July, 1666.

[8] *Ib.* 4 June, 1667.

[9] See *Catalogue of Pepysian MSS.*, i. 155.

[10] See *ib.* i. 156–7.

increased when the Third Dutch War broke out in the spring
of 1672. The Victuallers received such scanty payments from
the Government that they had to carry on the service with
their own money and credit[1], and eventually their condition
in respect of funds became 'so exceeding strait' that they
could not make proper deliveries[2]. This provoked the commanders at sea to take the field against them, and Prince
Rupert was so annoyed that he declared that he would never
thrive at sea till some were hanged on land[3]; and a little
later expressed the opinion that the only way to deal with
the Victuallers would be to send one of them on shipboard,
there to stay in what condition his Majesty shall think fitting,
till they have thoroughly victualled the fleet[4].

It is, on the whole, to the credit of the Victuallers that the
complaints as to quality are not more numerous than they
are during this period of large demands and scanty payment. If you would care for illustrations, on 15 March, 1671,
on board the *Reserve* 'there was a general complaint amongst
the seamen, both of the badness of the meat and want of
weight.'[5] On 6 September, 1672, there was a protest from
the *Gloucester* against the badness of the beer; but the Victuallers replied rather ambiguously that their beer was as
good as ever was used in the fleet, and they counted themselves happy in that they had been afflicted with less bad
beer 'by many degrees than ever was in such an action.'[6]
On 29 September the commander of the *Augustine* wrote
to say that the doctor attributed the sickness among his

---

[1] *Calendar of State Papers, Domestic,* 1671–2, pp. 66, 498.

[2] *Ib.* 1672, p. 484. For other references see pp. 31, 98, 106, 124, 453; and
ib. 1673, p. 72.

[3] *Ib.* 1673, p. xi.

[4] *Ib.* 1673, p. 384.

[5] *State Papers, Domestic, Charles II,* ccxcvii. 36. See also *Calendar of State
Papers, Domestic,* 1671, p. 135.

[6] *State Papers, Domestic, Charles II,* cccxxix. 11.

men to the extreme badness of the beer[1]; while objection was also taken to an untimely dispensation of rotten cheese[2].

The victualling contract of which we possess the fullest details was that of 31 December, 1677[3]. From this it appears that the daily allowance of each man was 'one pound averdupois of good, clean, sweet, sound, well-bolted with a horse-cloth, well-baked, and well-conditioned wheaten biscuit; one gallon, wine measure, of beer'...'two pounds averdupois of beef, killed and made up with salt in England, of a well-fed ox...for Sundays, Mondays, Tuesdays, and Thursdays'—or, instead of beef, for two of those days one pound averdupois of bacon, or salted English pork, of a well-fed hog...and a pint of pease (Winchester measure) therewith'...; 'and for Wednesdays, Fridays, and Saturdays, every man, besides the aforesaid allowance of bread and beer, to have by the day the eighth part of a full-sized North Sea cod of 24 inches long, or a sixth part of a haberdine 22 inches long, or a quarter part of the same sort if but 16 inches long...or a pound averdupois of well-savoured Poor John, together with two ounces of butter, and four ounces of Suffolk cheese, or two-thirds of that weight of Cheshire.' The contract provides for English beef because there was a strong prejudice in the navy against Irish beef. Pepys quotes one writer as saying 'The Irish meat is very unwholesome, as well as lean, and rots our men'[4]; and John Hollond argues that to serve Irish beef was greatly to discourage the seamen[5]. 'Haberdine' is salt or sun-dried cod, and 'Poor John' is salted or dried hake.

[1] *Calendar of State Papers, Domestic*, 1672, p. 668.

[2] *Ib.* 1672, p. 675. An interesting discussion of victualling abuses is contained in a paper of 1673 or 1674, entitled *The Expense and Charge of his Majesty's Naval Victuals considered and regulated*, by Captain Stephen Pyend or Pine, who had been himself formerly a purser (Pepysian MSS., *Miscellanies*, iii. 723). The substance of it is printed in *Catalogue of Pepysian MSS.*, i. 160–4.

[3] Pepysian MSS., No. 2867, *Naval Precedents*, p. 416. The contract is fully discussed in *Catalogue of Pepysian MSS.*, i. 165–177.

[4] Pepysian MSS., No. 2866, *Naval Minutes*, p. 146. [5] *Discourses*, p. 177.

In the case of vessels sailing 'to the southward of the latitude of 39 degrees N.' it was allowable for the contractors to vary the diet—' In lieu of a pound of biscuit, a pound of rusk of equal fineness; in lieu of a gallon of beer, a wine quart of beverage wine or half a wine pint of brandy...in lieu of a piece of beef or pork with pease, three pounds of flour and a pound of raisins (not worse than Malaga), or in lieu of raisins, half a pound of currants or half a pound of beef suet pickled; in lieu of a sized fish, four pounds of Milan rice or two stockfishes of at least 16 inches long; in lieu of a pound of butter or two pounds of Suffolk cheese, a wine pint of sweet olive oil.' The separate victualling contract for the Mediterranean[1] provided for this lighter diet there in any case; but the variation was not popular among the seamen. In Captain Boteler's *Six Dialogues about Sea Services*, printed in 1685 but written some fifty years earlier, the 'admiral,' who, having just been appointed to the 'high-admiralship,' is occupied throughout the book in remedying an abysmal ignorance of naval matters by conversation with a 'sea-captain,' suggests that it would be better for the health of the mariners if the ordinary victualling were assimilated 'to the manner of foreign parts.' 'Without doubt, my lord,' replies the captain, 'our much, and indeed excessive feeding upon these salt meats at sea cannot but procure much unhealthiness and infection, and is questionless one main cause that our English are so subject to calentures, scarbots, and the like contagious diseases above all other nations; so that it were to be wished that we did more conform ourselves, if not to the Spanish and Italian nations, who live most upon rice-meal, oatmeal, biscake, figs, olives, oil, and the like, yet at the least to our neighbours the Dutch, who content themselves with a far less proportion of flesh and fish than we do, and instead thereof do make it up with pease, beans, wheat-

---

[1] Described in *Catalogue of Pepysian MSS.*, i. 177.

flour, butter, cheese, and those white meats (as they are called).' To this view the admiral assents, but he adds, 'The difficulty consisteth in that the common seamen with us are so besotted on their beef and pork as they had rather adventure on all the calentures and scarbots in the world than to be weaned from their customary diet, or so much as to lose the least bit of it.' I should explain that a calenture is a fever, associated with delirium, to which sailors in the tropics were peculiarly liable ; and scarbot is the scurvy[1].

Pepys expected much from the new contract of 1677[2], but the old complaints of delay and bad quality recur[3], and in 1683 his successors decided to abandon contract in favour of a state victualling department resembling in its general character the system of victualling 'upon account,'[4] established from 1655 to the Restoration. If we may infer anything from the silence of the *Admiralty Letters*, hitherto so vocal upon the subject, this change of method resulted in an improvement in the victualling of the navy, and on the whole the Victualling Office did not come out badly under the test of the mobilisation of 1688. The necessity for this had been realised about the middle of August, and at first the delays caused a good deal of anxiety; but by the end of October Pepys was able to report that the fleet is 'now (God be thanked) at the Gunfleet, and in very good condition there.'[5]

---

[1] 'Calentures,' or burning fevers, were supposed to be bred by calms. Sir Walter Ralegh refers to his own sufferings from them (*Remains*, London, 1664, p. 223).

'Scarbot' is probably from 'scharbock,' the Danish name for one form of scurvy (John Quincey, *Lexicon Physico-medicum*, London, 1787); the modern Danish term for scurvy is 'skabet.'   [2] See *Admiralty Letters*, vi. 228.

[3] Instances are given in *Catalogue of Pepysian MSS.*, i. 179–80.

[4] A discussion of the relative merits of the two systems occurs in Hollond, *Discourses*, p. 154. The substance of the patent of 10 December, 1683 (*Naval Precedents*, p. 48), which established the new department, is given in *Catalogue of Pepysian MSS.*, pp. 180–2.

[5] Pepysian MSS., *Admiralty Letters*, xv. 250 (26 Oct). See also pp. 219–20, 256–7, 284.

There were still ships waiting to be got ready for sea, but of these he writes: 'I do with the same zeal continue to press the despatch of the rest that are behind that I would do for my victuals if I were hungry.'[1]

One of the earlier acts of the Restoration Government was the passing of a statute to incorporate into the system of English law the ordinances already in force during the Interregnum for regulating the discipline of the navy. Before 1652 such crimes as murder and manslaughter on board ship had been punishable by the ordinary law, and lesser offences by the 'known orders and customs of the seas'[2]; but in that year the service was for the first time subjected to articles of war[3], and it was upon these that the provisions of the Act of 1661[4] were founded. By this commanders at sea were empowered to try a great variety of offences by court-martial, and for many of these the maximum penalty was death. This Act continued to govern the navy until the reign of George II.

Another Act, of 1664[5], dealt with two matters which had given a great deal of trouble to the Navy Board—the frequent embezzlement of naval stores, and the riots among disappointed seamen who could not get their pay. Efforts had been already made to prevent embezzlement by adopting special modes of manufacture for the King's rope, sails, and pennants, and by marking other stores with the broad arrow[6]; but there were some things, such as nails and some

[1] Pepysian MSS., *Admiralty Letters*, xv. 241.
[2] See Pepysian MSS., No. 2611, *Penn's Collections*, p. 95: 'Instructions for the Admiralty, 1647.' These customs were not abrogated, either by the ordinances of the Interregnum or by the statutes of the Restoration.
[3] Oppenheim, p. 311.
[4] 13 Car. II. c. 9. A summary of the provisions of the Act is given in *Catalogue of Pepysian MSS.*, i. 184.
[5] 16 Car. II. c. 5; renewed by 18 & 19 Car. II. c. 12.
[6] *Calendar of State Papers, Domestic*, 1661–2, p. 152.

other kinds of ironwork, which could not be thus marked. Ironwork in particular was especially favoured by the depredators, because it could be so easily disposed of. In August, 1663, an illicit storehouse discovered at Deptford for the reception of nails, iron shot, and other embezzled ironwork, was described as the 'gulf that swallows up all from any place brought to him.'[1] The riots also had been a serious matter. The preamble of the Act gives as the ground of legislation 'diverse fightings, quarrellings, and disturbances ...in and about his Majesty's offices, yards, and stores,' and 'frequent differences and disorders' which had occurred on pay-days through 'the unreasonable turbulency of seamen.' To meet this state of things the Act invests the Navy Board with some of the powers of magistrates, and authorises them to punish riots and embezzlements with fine and imprisonment.

The Act was useful, but it did not entirely stop embezzlement. In September, 1666, a prize worth £300 was plundered of her lading, and 'will soon,' we are told, 'be dismantled of all her rigging, till she will not have a rope's end left to hang herself, or the thievish seamen that go in her.'[2] Chatham Harbour had always been 'miserably infested' with 'thieves and pilfering rogues,'[3] and in February, 1668, the clerk of the check wrote, 'our people's hands are of late so inured to stealing, that if the sawyers leave any work in the pits half cut, it's a hazard whether they find it in the morning.'[4] The state of things complained of was partly due to the uncertainty of pay. As far as the riots of seamen were concerned, the Act was a failure, as for their grievances force was no

---

[1] *Calendar of State Papers, Domestic*, 1663-4, p. 249.

[2] *Ib.* 1666-7, p. 148.

[3] *State Papers, Domestic, Charles II*, ccxvii. 138.

[4] *Ib.* ccxxxv. 135. See also *Calendar of State Papers, Domestic*, 1668-9, pp. 171, 303; *ib.* 1671, pp. 523, 524.

remedy. Pepys writes on 4 November, 1665[1], when the Act of 1664 was in full operation, 'After dinner I to the Office and there late, and much troubled to have a hundred seamen all the afternoon there, swearing below and cursing us, and breaking the glass windows, and swear they will pull the house down on Tuesday next. I sent word of this to Court, but nothing will help it but money and a rope.'

The period of Pepys's first Secretaryship witnessed several attempts to effect an improvement in naval discipline. Abuses connected with the unlimited number of cabins built on the King's ships, leading to 'the pestering of the ship,' 'contracting of sickness,' temptation to officers 'to neglect their duties and mis-spend their time in drinking and debauchery,' and 'the danger of fire,' led to the adoption, on 16 October, 1673, of a regular establishment of cabins for ships of each rate[2].

Another abuse of long standing had been the taking of merchants' goods in the King's ships. Sir Robert Slyngesbie had observed in his *Discourse*[3] in 1660 that this made it easy for the officers to sell the King's stores under the pretence that they were merchandise; to waste time in the ports which ought to have been spent at sea; and so to fill the ship's hold 'that they have no room to throw by their chests and other cumbersome things upon occasion of fight, whereby the gun decks are so encumbered that they cannot possibly make so good an opposition to an enemy as otherwise they might'; and, lastly, to defraud the custom-house. In 1674 Pepys took the matter up, and induced the King to take severe notice of the offenders[4], and in one particularly

---

[1] *Diary.* See also the entries for 19 October, 1666, and 25 June, 1667; and p. 45, *supra.*

[2] Pepysian MSS., No. 2867, *Naval Precedents,* pp. 525–8. The establishment is printed in *Catalogue of Pepysian MSS.,* i. 189–92.

[3] Hollond, *Discourses,* p. 353. Macaulay describes the abuse, but is silent concerning the attempts to remedy it (*History of England,* i. 148).

[4] Pepysian MSS., *Admiralty Letters,* iii. 367.

flagrant case of 1675 to offer the delinquent commander the alternative of imprisonment until trial by court-martial, or forfeiting the whole of his pay for the voyage, and 'making good to the poor of the Chest' at Chatham out of his own purse the value of the freight of the merchants' goods brought home by him[1].

The absence of commanders from their ships without leave gave a good deal of trouble during the period 1673–9. On 1 October, 1673, the Commissioners of the Admiralty ordered that the commanders should be 'pricked out of pay' for such absences[2]; but on 25 May, 1675, Pepys observes 'with much trouble' that the 'late resolutions' 'are already forgotten,' commanders 'appearing daily in the town' without leave[3]. On 9 July he 'spied' the captain of the *Lark* 'at a distance sauntering up and down Covent Garden, as I have too often heretofore observed him spending his time when the King's service required his attendance on shipboard, as it doth at this day—a practice which shall never pass my knowledge in any commander (be he who he will) without my taking notice of it to his Majesty and my Lords of the Admiralty.'[4] Three years later complaints of this kind became very frequent, and so to the end of Pepys's first Secretaryship in 1679. On 24 March, 1678, he writes: 'I must confess I have never observed so frequent and scandalous instances as I do at this day by commanders hovering daily about the Court and town, though without the least pretence for it.'[5] 'I would to God,' he writes on 29 June to Sir Thomas Allin, 'you could offer me something that may be an effectual cure to the liberty taken by commanders of leaving their ships upon pretence of private occasions, and staying long in town, to the great dishonour of his Majesty's service, and corrupting

---

[1] Pepysian MSS., *Admiralty Letters*, iv. 233, 243, 246.
[2] *Ib.* ii. 182. [3] *Ib.* iv. 110.
[4] *Ib.* iv. 178. [5] *Ib.* vi. 480.

the discipline of the Navy by their example...it seeming impossible as well as unreasonable to keep the door constantly barred against commanders' desires of coming to town upon just and pressing occasions of their families, and of the other hand no less hard upon the King that his gracious nature as well as his service should be always liable to be imposed upon by commanders, as often as their humours, pleasures, or (it may be) vices shall incline them to come ashore. Pray think of it and help me herein, for, as I shall never be guilty of withstanding any gentleman's just occasions and desires in this matter, so I shall never be able to sit still and silent under the scandalous liberties that I see every day taken by commanders of playing with his Majesty's service, as if it were an indifferent matter whether they give any attendance on board their ships, so as they have their wages as if they did.'[1]

The official correspondence of 1673–9, although it reveals a grievous laxity of discipline[2], exhibits Pepys himself in a favourable light. He had a high sense of the honour of the service, and shewed himself both firm and humane in his dealings with his official inferiors. He was at great pains to keep himself informed of the proceedings of the commanders, and when breaches of discipline were reported to him, he took infinite trouble to arrive at the facts. His admonitions to the offenders, though sometimes a little unctuous, are as a rule in the best Pepysian style.

The decay of discipline in the Restoration period has been associated by some writers with the practice of appointing 'gentlemen captains' without experience to important

[1] Pepysian MSS., *Admiralty Letters*, vii. 296.

[2] Pepys, in a letter of 3 February, 1674, addressed to Captain Rooth, refers to 'the universal loss of discipline amongst the seamen of England,' 'a vice which I pray God grant I may see rectified before it prove too fatal, not only to his Majesty's service, but to the whole navigation of the country' (*Admiralty Letters*, iii. 78).

commands at sea. The matter is discussed by Macaulay, picturesquely but with exaggeration[1]; Pepys, in the *Diary*, quotes Coventry as referring to the 'unruliness' of the 'young gentlemen captains'[2] and confessing 'that the more of the cavaliers are put in, the less of discipline hath followed in the fleet'[3]; and a Restoration paper printed in Charnock's *Marine Architecture*[4] very much shocks that author by its 'illiberal and improper observations' on the subject. He admits, however, that 'there certainly appears much truth and solidity in the general principle of them,' though 'it might have been wished for the sake of decency and propriety' that the writer 'had conveyed his animadversions in somewhat less vulgar terms.' The victim of Charnock's criticism traces every kind of evil to the year 1660, when 'gentlemen came to command in the navy.' These 'have had the honour to bring drinking, gaming, whoring, swearing, and all impiety into the navy, and banish all order and sobriety out of their ships'; they have cast their ships away for want of seamanship[5]; they have habitually delayed in port when they should have been at sea; a gentleman captain will bring 'near twenty landmen into the ship as his footmen, tailor, barber, fiddlers, decayed kindred, volunteer gentlemen or acquaintance, as companions,' and these 'are of Bishop Williams's opinion, that Providence made man to live ashore, and it is necessity that drives him to sea.' The writer concludes that 'the Crown will at all times be better able to secure trade, prevent the growth of the naval strength of our enemy, with £100,000 under a natural sea admiralty and seamen captains...than with three times that sum under land admirals and gentlemen captains not bred tarpaulins.'

[1] *History of England*, i. 147–9.   [2] *Diary*, 27 July, 1666.
[3] *Diary*, 2 June, 1663. *Cf.* also 10 January, 20 October, 1666; 29 June, 1667.
[4] Vol. i. pp. lxxiv–xcv.
[5] *Cf. Diary*, 28 October, 1666.

With some qualifications this is the view of Pepys. He disclaims hostility to gentlemen captains as such; but he quotes from a speech delivered by Colonel Birch in the House of Commons, in which he had urged that one of the 'present miscarriages' of the navy is that 'employment and favour are now bestowed wholly upon gentlemen, to the great discouragement of tarpaulins of Wapping and Blackwall, from whence...the good commanders of old were all used to be chosen.'[1] Pepys also refers to the liberty taken by gentlemen commanders of 'thinking themselves above the necessity of obeying orders, and conforming themselves to the rules and discipline of the Navy, in reliance upon the protection secured to them therein through the quality of their friends at Court.'[2] Pepys himself was probably an impartial witness, for he was denounced by each side for favouring the other[3].

It is in a way remarkable that during the period of complaints against gentlemen captains we come upon the first establishment of an examination for lieutenants. Towards the end of 1677 complaints reached the Admiralty from Sir John Narbrough, commanding in the Mediterranean, of the 'defectiveness' of his lieutenants 'in their seamanship.'[4] Pepys also refers to 'the general ignorance and dulness of our lieutenants of ships' as 'a great evil' of which 'all sober commanders at this day' complain. They are 'for the most part (at least those of later standing) made out of volunteers, who having passed some time superficially at sea, and being related to families of interest at Court, do obtain lieutenancies before they are fitted for it.'[5] The result was the adoption on 18 December of a regular establishment[6], drawn up by

---

[1] Letter to Sir John Holmes, 15 April, 1679 (Pepysian. MSS., *Admiralty Letters*, ix. 206).

[2] Letter to the same, 18 April, 1679 (*ib.* ix. 214).

[3] *Ib.* ix. 242–3.   [4] *Ib.* vi. 231.

[5] Letter to Sir John Kempthorne, 1 December, 1677 (*ib.* vi. 264).

[6] Pepysian MSS., No. 2867, *Naval Precedents*, p. 241.

Pepys[1], 'for ascertaining the duty of a sea-lieutenant, and for examining persons pretending to that office.' A lieutenant was required to have served three years actually at sea; to be 20 years of age at least; to produce 'good certificates' from the commanders under whom he had served of his 'sobriety, diligence, obedience to order,' and 'application to the study and practice of the art of navigation,' as well as three further certificates—from a member of the Navy Board who had served as a commander, from a flag officer, and from a commander of a first or second rate—'upon a solemn examination,' held at the Navy Office, of 'his ability to judge of and perform the duty of an able seaman and midshipman, and his having attained to a sufficient degree of knowledge in the theory of navigation capacitating him thereto.' Candidates were sometimes ploughed[2], and this, as Pepys points out, was an encouragement to the 'true-bred seaman' and greatly to the benefit of the King's service. 'I thank God,' he writes in 1678[3], 'we have not half the throng of those of the bastard breed pressing for employments which we heretofore used to be troubled with, they being conscious of their inability to pass this examination, and know it to be to no purpose now to solicit for employments till they have done it.'

To about the same time as the examination for lieutenants belongs another minor reform—an establishment for the better provision of naval chaplains. In April or May, 1677, the King and Lords of the Admiralty resolved 'that no persons shall be entertained as chaplains on board his Majesty's ships but such as shall be approved of by the Lord Bishop of London.'[4] The proposal originated in the first instance with Pepys, who designed it to remedy 'the ill-effects of the looseness wherein that matter lay, with respect both to the

---

[1] *Admiralty Letters*, vi. 256. [2] *Ib.* vii. 4.
[3] In a letter of 29 March, 1678 (*ib.* vii. 17). [4] *Ib.* vi. 3.

honour of God Almighty and the preservation of sobriety and good discipline in his Majesty's fleet.'[1] The details of the scheme were more fully worked out by resolutions adopted by the Admiralty Commission on 15 December, 1677[2].

An important measure which had an indirect bearing upon discipline was James II's 'establishment about plate carriage and allowance for captains' tables,'[3] dated 15 July, 1686. The title of the establishment gives little indication of its real scope; it was designed to give the Admiralty a better control over ships on foreign service, and at the same time so to improve the position of the commanders as to put them beyond the reach of temptations to neglect their public duty for private gain. The preamble refers to the 'general disorder' into which the discipline of the navy has 'of late years' fallen, and especially to the particular evil arising from 'the liberty taken by commanders of our ships (upon all opportunities of private profit) of converting the service of our said ships to their own use, and the total neglect of the public ends for which they, at our great charge, are set forth and maintained, namely, the annoying of our enemies, the protecting the estates of our trading subjects, and the support of our honour with foreign princes.' Commanders are accordingly forbidden to convey money, jewels, merchandise, or passengers without the King's warrant; and copies of orders given by admirals or commanders-in-chief are to be sent to the Secretary of the Admiralty, as also interim reports of proceedings, and a complete journal at

---

[1] *Admiralty Letters*, vi. 18, 45. See also vi. 19 and *Naval Minutes*, p. 81.

[2] Pepysian MSS., No. 2867, *Naval Precedents*, p. 161. The substance of these resolutions is given in *Catalogue of Pepysian MSS.*, i. 206. See also there the new instructions of 20 October, 1685, for the guard-boats in Chatham and Portsmouth harbours (i. 208).

[3] Pepysian MSS., No. 2867, *Naval Precedents*, p. 245. Printed in Pepys's *Memoires* (Oxford reprint), pp. 55–68.

the end of the voyage. In consideration of these requirements, commanders are to receive substantial additional allowances 'for the support of their tables,' ranging from £83 a year to £250 according to the ship's rate.

The reign of James II was in a peculiar degree a period of the framing and revising of 'establishments,' and on 13 April, 1686, a new establishment was made concerning 'volunteers and midshipmen extraordinary.'[1] This appears to be a confirmation of an earlier establishment of 4 May, 1676, designed to afford encouragement 'to families of better quality...to breed up their younger sons to the art and practice of navigation' by 'the bearing several young gentlemen, to the ends aforesaid' on board the King's ships as 'volunteers,' and to provide employment for ex-commanders or lieutenants by carrying them as 'midshipmen extraordinary' over and above the ordinary complement assigned to the ship in which they sailed. Another 'establishment' of the same period is that of November, 1686, for boatswains' and carpenters' sea stores[2].

During the earlier part of Pepys's second Secretaryship, drunkenness gave a good deal of trouble. For instance, in 1685 the commander of the *Diamond* complained that his officers were 'sottish, and unfit to serve the King,' particularly the gunner, who was 'dead drunk in his cabin when the powder was to be taken out.'[3] Pepys refers on 5 August, 1684, to 'the generality of that vice, now running through the whole navy,'[4] and on 4 February, 1685, he writes, 'Till that vice be cured, which I find too far spread in the navy, both by sea and land, I do despair of ever seeing his Majesty's service therein to thrive, and as I have given one or two

---

[1] Pepysian MSS., No. 2867, *Naval Precedents*, p. 156.

[2] *Ib.* p. 639. Both these establishments are more fully described in *Catalogue of Pepysian MSS.*, pp. 213–16.

[3] *Admiralty Letters*, xi. 372.　　　　　[4] *Ib.* x. 89.

instances of my care therein already, so shall I not fail by the
grace of God to persevere in it, as far as I am able, till it be
thoroughly cured, let it light where it will.'¹ In these efforts
the Secretary of the Admiralty was soon to be powerfully
supported by the new King, 'there being no one vice,'
Pepys writes on 15 February, 1685, 'which can give more
just occasion of offence to his Majesty than that of drunkenness, for the restraining which, as well in the navy as in
every other part of the service, I well know he has immove-
ably determined to have the severest means used, nor shall
I in my station fail (according to his commands and my
duty) to give my helping hand thereto.'²

In connexion with discipline it may be mentioned that
even as early as the Restoration there were labour troubles
in the dockyards. In 1663 a separate room was applied for in
the new storehouse at Portsmouth for use as a workroom,
'as seamen and carpenters will never agree to work together.'³
In the same year the clerk of the Portsmouth ropeyard complained of the workmen employed there. By hasty spinning
they finished what they called a day's work by dinner-time,
and then refused to work again till four o'clock. 'Yesterday,'
he writes, 'about twenty-five of them left the work to go to
the alehouse, where, I think, they remain.'⁴ On 26 March,
1664, the shipwrights and caulkers at Deptford are complained of because they work very slowly, and 'give ill
language' when pressed to work⁵. Later on, in January,
1671, Commissioner John Cox appears to have had almost
as much trouble with the master workmen and their instru-
ments in Chatham dockyard. They were remiss in their

¹ *Admiralty Letters*, x. 310.   ² *Ib.* x. 331.
³ *State Papers, Domestic, Charles II*, lxix. 43.
⁴ *Ib.* lxxviii. 105. See also *Calendar of State Papers, Domestic*, 1663-4,
pp. 244 and 276.
⁵ *State Papers, Domestic, Charles II*, xcv. 147.

attendance, and met his efforts at their amendment by passive resistance[1].

The two great shipbuilding years of our period were 1666 and 1679—the first accounted for by the Second Dutch War, and the latter by the Act of 1677 for thirty new ships to which I have already referred[2]. How much was done during the Restoration period to strengthen the navy on its material side can be realised by a comparison made in tabular form in Pepys's *Register of Ships*[3]. In 1660 the navy consisted of 156 vessels, in 1688 of 173; but a comparison of numbers gives no adequate idea of relative strength. In 1660 there were only 3 first rates as against 9 in 1688; second rates, 11 at both dates; third rates, 16 against 39; fourth rates, 45 against 41; fifth rates, 37 against 2; sixth rates, 23 against 6—shewing that the tendency had been to build bigger ships. In 1660 there were only 30 ships of the first three rates, but in 1688 the number was nearly doubled, rising to 59. Another feature in the table is the development of the fireship and the yacht[4]. In 1660 there were no fireships in the navy; in 1688, 26. In 1660 there was one yacht, and in 1688 there were 14. The strength of the fleet may also be tested in another way, by comparing tonnage, men, and guns[5]. In 1660 the tonnage was 62,594; in 1688, 101,032. In 1660 the number of men borne on the sea establishment was 19,551; in 1688, 41,940. In 1660 the total number of guns was 4,642; in 1688, 6,954.

[1] *Calendar of State Papers, Domestic*, 1671, p. 44.

[2] p. 31, *supra*. A list of these ships is printed in *Catalogue of Pepysian MSS.*, i. 223.

[3] *Ib.* i. 304. The whole of Pepys's *Register*, with a number of illustrative tables, is printed there on pp. 253–306; as also his *Register of Sea-Commission Officers* on pp. 307–435.

[4] Another novelty of the period is the revival of the galley in the English navy. This is fully discussed in *ib.* i. 227–8.

[5] *Ib.* i. 306.

In connexion with guns, the important achievement of the period was the systematising, under the methodical hand of Pepys, of the arrangements for determining the number and type of the armament of each rate, and the number of men required to work it. In 1677 he drew up a 'general establishment' of men and guns[1], and this was officially adopted as 'a solemn, universal, and unalterable adjustment of the gunning and manning of the whole fleet[2].'

Let me now sum up briefly our general conclusions.

In the light of the facts which I have endeavoured to set out in these lectures, the old notion that the naval administration of the Interregnum was pious and efficient and that of the Restoration immoral and slack appears crude and unsatisfying. But there is this element of truth in it—that vigorous efforts for the regeneration of the navy were to a certain extent rendered abortive by the corruption of the Court and the lowness of the prevailing political tone. Able and energetic reformers were baffled by want of money, and this was due partly to royal extravagance and partly to unsatisfactory relations with Parliament, which suspected peculation and waste. Discipline also was undermined by the introduction into the service of unfit persons, who obtained admission and were protected from the adequate punishment of their delinquencies by the interest of persons of quality at Court. Further, an atmosphere was created which enervated some of the reformers themselves. It is remarkable that in spite of these drawbacks so much should have been accomplished. The facts and figures contained in the naval manuscripts in the Pepysian Library go a long

---

[1] Pepysian MSS., No. 2866, *Naval Minutes*, p. 61.

[2] Pepysian MSS., *Admiralty Letters*, vi. 201–2. This establishment is given in Pepysian MSS., No. 2867, *Naval Precedents*, p. 202, and the tables there given are printed and fully discussed in *Catalogue of Pepysian MSS.*, i. 234–42. See also pp. 242–4 for the reorganisation of the Office of the Ordnance in 1683.

way to justify the claims made by Pepys on behalf of the administrations with which he himself was connected, and particularly on behalf of the Special Commission of 1686, which, as he says, 'raised the Navy of England from the lowest state of impotence to the most advanced step towards a lasting and solid prosperity that (all circumstances considered) this nation had ever seen it at.'[1] The characteristic vices of the Restoration, as he describes them, are all there— 'the laziness of one, the private business or love of pleasure in another, want of method in a third, and zeal to the affair in most'—but except during the period 1679 to 1684 there was no abject incompetence and some steady progress. Even Charles II understood 'the business of the sea,'[2] 'possessed a transcendent mastery in all maritime knowledge,'[3] and when he was acting as Lord High Admiral transacted a good deal of naval business with his own hand[4]. James II was a real authority upon shipbuilding[5], took an interest in the details of administration[6], recognised the importance of discipline, and might have restored it if destiny had not intervened. But much more is to be attributed to the methodical industry of their great subordinate, and to his 'daily eye and hand' upon all departments of naval affairs. His vitality of character and variety of interests appear in the *Diary*, but from his official correspondence we get something different; for in a document which is so true to human nature as the *Diary*, it is almost inevitable that the diarist, although sufficiently self-satisfied, should be quite unconscious of his strongest points. We should expect business habits in a Government official, but in his correspondence Pepys ex-

---

[1] *Memoires* (Oxford reprint), p. 130.
[2] Pepysian MSS., No. 2866, *Naval Minutes*, p. 76.
[3] Derrick, *Memoirs of the Royal Navy*, p. 84.
[4] For instances of this see *Catalogue of Pepysian MSS.*, i. 246 nn.
[5] Pepysian MSS., *Admiralty Letters*, xi. 200; xii. 71, 91, 200; xiii. 23.
[6] *Catalogue of Pepysian MSS.*, i. 247 n.

hibits a methodical devotion to business which is beyond
praise. We have here sobriety and soundness of judgment;
a sense of the paramount importance of discipline, and the
exercise of a steady pressure upon others to restore it in the
navy; a high standard of personal duty, which permits no
slackness and spares no pains; and a remarkable capacity
for tactful diplomacy. The decorous self-satisfaction of the
Diary has been replaced in later years by professional pride;
and an outlook upon business affairs which had always been
intelligent, has become profoundly serious. The agreeable
vices of the *Diary* suggest the light irresponsible cavalier.
The official correspondence suggests that Pepys was a Puritan at heart, although without the Puritan rigidity of practice
or narrowness of view. In his professional career he exhibits
precisely those virtues which had made the naval administration of Blake's time a success—the virtues of the Inde-
pendent colonels who manned the administrative offices
during the First Dutch War. The change is that from the
rather dissolute-looking young Royalist painted by Lely
about 1669 to the ample wig and pursed official lips of the
later portrait by Kneller[1].

It is not surprising that a man so observant, so experienced,
and so absorbed in the navy should have drawn the moral
of the naval history of his own time. In his *Memoires of the
Royal Navy*[2], the only work which he ever acknowledged[3],
Pepys states the essential 'truths' of the 'sea œconomy' of
England, which are as valid to-day as when he wrote them
down—'that integrity and general (but unpractised) knowledge are not alone sufficient to conduct and support a Navy

----

[1] Both these portraits are at Magdalene College, the former in the Hall and
the latter in the Library.

[2] Oxford reprint, p. 130.

[3] *The Portugal History, or a Relation of the Troubles that happened in the
Court of Portugal in the years* 1667 *and* 1668...*by S. P. esq.* (1677) has also
been attributed to him.

so as to prevent its declension into a state little less unhappy than the worst that can befall it under the want of both'; 'that not much more (neither) is to be depended on even from experience alone and integrity, unaccompanied with vigour of application, assiduity, affection, strictness of discipline, and method'; but that what is really needed is 'a strenuous conjunction of all these.' For himself he claims due credit, for it was 'a strenuous conjunction of all these (and that conjunction only)' that redeemed the navy in 1686.

An anonymous admirer[1] wrote of Pepys as 'the great treasurer of naval and maritime knowledge,' who was 'aequi-ponderous' to his colleagues 'in moral, and much superior in philosophical knowledge and the universal knowledge of the œconomy of the navy.' Modern eulogies are phrased more simply, but we may fairly claim for this great public servant that he did more than anyone else under a King who hated 'the very sight or thoughts of business'[2] to apply business principles to naval administration.

---

[1] *Letter to the Earl of Marlborough*, by T. H., possibly Thomas Hayter, Pepys's clerk, who succeeded him in 1673 as Clerk of the Acts.
[2] *Diary*, 15 May, 1663.

INDEX

Trinity House, 3
Turenne, 22

Victualling, 57–64; abuses in, 5, 9;
victualling 'upon account,' 10, 57,
63; contract of 1677, 61; contract
for the Mediterranean, 62
Volunteers, establishments for (1676
and 1686), 73

Wages, abuses in, 6; tickets for, 7,
47, 53; 'dead pays,' 7, 54

Wapping, 70
Warren, Sir William, timber con-
tractor, 28
Warwick, Sir Philip, 40
Watermen's Hall, 46, 47
Weymouth, 49
Wounded seamen, scale of relief
for (1685), 51; *see also* Sick and
Wounded

Yachts, 75
Yarmouth, 49

For EU product safety concerns, contact us at Calle de José Abascal, 56–1°,
28003 Madrid, Spain or eugpsr@cambridge.org.

www.ingramcontent.com/pod-product-compliance
Ingram Content Group UK Ltd.
Pitfield, Milton Keynes, MK11 3LW, UK
UKHW010049140625
459647UK00012BB/1704